Childhood trauma, we now know, plays out in disastrous lifelong ways. In this achingly brave, compassionate, searching, and lyrical memoir, Cinthia Ritchie shows how a seemingly bucolic country childhood can be fraught with danger and that family secrets and silences wall off even close siblings from one another. Ritchie's beautifully written and deeply felt story about "a family afraid to tell the truth" succeeds at last in sorting truth from lies as it demonstrates the strengths and vulnerabilities of survivors.
—Nancy Lord, former Alaska Writer Laureate, author of *Fishcamp: Life on an Alaskan Shore* and *pH: A Novel*

Cinthia Ritchie writes lyrically and courageously about suffering, hunger, and abuse in all its forms, and about love, too. It hurt me to read this book, but I'm glad she wrote it, as I'm sure it will save someone's life.
—**Heather Lende, author of** *Take Good Care of the Garden and the Dogs*

The stakes are high in Cinthia Ritchie's brave memoir *Malnourished: A Memoir of Sisterhood and Hunger*. Exploring one's loss, grief, guilt, and love is dangerous; it can take one to the edge of the tolerable and into deep despair. But as Ritchie slowly and intentionally pulls back the curtains of her childhood, her vivid and compelling voice carries us through each thrust and parry ultimately bringing us closer and closer to the most unbearable of all, her sister's death from anorexia starvation. It may be the case, as Joan Didion wrote in *The White Album*, that "we look for the sermon in the suicide," but there is no sermon here. Instead, we get to experience in this achingly beautiful book the healing that comes from putting the narrative into words.
—**Ronald Spatz, editor,** *Alaska Quarterly Review*

At times pure poetry, at times as searing as a lightning bolt, *Malnourished* is the kind of book that sticks with you long after you've read it. Told by the sister who survived, it is a haunting journey that forces the reader to confront the reality of abuse, society's expectations for young women, and, ultimately, the strength it takes to escape the past. Quite simply, the unflinching honesty and the beauty of the writing left me breathless.

—**Mary Emerick, author of** *The Geography of Water* **and** *Fire in the Heart: A Memoir of Friendship, Loss, and Wildfire*

Powered by a courageous appetite for understanding, Cinthia Ritchie's *Malnourished* explores raw truths about love, identity, sisterhood, and survival, inviting readers to inhabit an ultimately resilient woman's complex longings.

—**Andromeda Romano-Lax, author of** *Plum Rains* **and** *The Spanish Bow*

MALNOURISHED

MALNOURISHED

A Memoir of Sisterhood

and Hunger

CINTHIA RITCHIE

RAISED VOICE PRESS
Clearwater, Florida

Copyright © 2019 by Cinthia Ritchie

Published by Raised Voice Press
PO Box 14502
Clearwater, Florida 33766
www.raisedvoicepress.com

All rights reserved. No part of this book may be reproduced without
the publisher's written permission, except for brief quotations
in reviews.

Author photo by Michael Mitchell
Cover design by Sarah Flood-Baumann
Interior design by Karen Pickell

Published in the United States of America

ISBN 978-1-949259-06-3 (Paperback)
ISBN 978-1-949259-07-0 (Ebook–Kindle)
ISBN 978-1-949259-08-7 (Ebook–EPUB)

Library of Congress Control Number: 2019948176

Portions of this book were previously published, in different form, in
Mary: A Journal of New Writing, *The Hunger*, and *Water-Stone Review*.

for Cathie

MALNOURISHED

PROLOGUE

Anchorage, Alaska

Even though I hadn't been born yet, I still remember my second-oldest sister's birth, my mother carrying her home from the hospital wrapped in a blue blanket because she was only the second and my father still had hopes for a boy. The light in the living room hazy and soft, since it was the beginning of March and twilight only lasted a few moments. We stood around, my oldest sister and I, we stood at the legs of our father, his pants dark and wrinkled and smelling of tobacco and dust, and we strained our toes, trying to make ourselves taller.

My mother leaned down and held Deena in front of us, and she was so small, her face pinched in disapproval, her tiny hands punching. The corner of her mouth turned down slightly so that she looked both young and old, wise and unknowing.

She stunned me, this sister of mine with the wizened face and the angry fists. I wanted to touch her but kept my arms straight at my sides, elbows locked and stubborn. It was as if I knew, even then, that she would balk at receiving affection, that this was the one grace she would never quite master.

Spring in Alaska creeps slowly, birch trees pale and bare and then, without warning, tiny buds sprouting until there is green, such a bright and hopeful green that it almost hurts to witness.

Deena didn't die in the spring, but I always think of her then because she was so closed, so hidden, she kept to herself, slept all day in a series of shabby apartments, coming out only at night, talking to no one but her dog.

I didn't know she lived like that, though maybe I did. Probably I did.

What happened next was as much my fault as hers, which simply means that you can be swept away, willingly and with abandon. This is what happened to Deena, and to me. We fell. Down in the grass, in the green and damp grass.

There can be worse ways to go, Cin, she whispers to me.

That's a lie. There was no whisper, no voice. I made that up to make myself feel better.

～⌇～

I eat grass. I prefer clover but also like flowers, violets, chamomile buds, and the sharp and bitter tang of dandelion greens.

Sometimes when I'm hiking, I place small stones in my mouth, suck off the dirt, run my tongue over the edges, the indentations, the tiny ridges.

It's impossible to keep things out of my mouth.

～⌇～

When my son was younger, we used to drive out to Turnagain Arm and wait for the beluga whales, which arrived on the late summer tides to feed on salmon. We stood on rocks above the shore, we stood in rain and sun, waiting for those ghost-white bodies and when we spotted one, our chests fluttered as we watched it lift up out of the water, back gleaming, tail flicking. It was like being inside a movie, surreal and magical. Once, we looked up to find a beluga whale swimming alongside the beach. Up close, it was more of a grayish shade, more ordinary and yet more majestic than when glimpsed from a distance.

Memory is a funny thing, isn't it, how it adds and subtracts, takes something as simple as watching a whale swim along the shore and mixes it up in your mind so that your sister is there beside you, even though she's been dead for years. Still, this is what you remember: the wind and the smell of the marsh, the silver-blue tint of an Alaska twilight spreading the water, and beyond it all, the small and simple feel of your dead sister's hand slipping inside of yours.

What else can you possibly do? You tighten your grip. You hold on.

STARVING

―∽·͡―

Words from the Dead

I am drowning, that is what this is, but she felt no terror, only a calm and almost logical tranquility, as if the waters had risen over her head already and she had only to acknowledge them, and die.

I am not drowning, really. I will swim free.

—stolen copied from Deena's notebooks

Northwestern Pennsylvania

At night, the sky fell down and smothered me, stars in my mouth and skin. The moon swimming my blood. I could fly at such times. I could lift my thin arms and soar.

———◦◦———

Growing up in northwestern Pennsylvania, Deena and I were inseparable. Her smells and tastes surrounded me, and when she cut her finger on a rock, I licked it clean, her blood lingering for a moment on my tongue before I swallowed. All summer we roamed the fields and woods, swam in the pond, built bridges and forts across the creek. Our legs scabby, shorts old and frayed, shoes with holes in the toes. It never occurred to us to care about how we looked, not when we were outside with the land and trees and sky.

We liked to play games about church. We were intrigued by religion, by the priest and the Mass and the heady, suffocating smell of incense. We placed small stones on each other's tongues and pretended they were communion wafers. "The body of Christ. Amen." Giggling and clapping our hands over our mouths because it was so preposterous: a girl, a female, delivering the host.

Kneeling in the pasture, wreaths of clover in our hair, hands folded as if in prayer. We were adamant that we would never marry or have children, we were confident that we would never end up like our mother; the idea was ridiculous, crazy. We had big plans: To move out West and become cowboys. To run away to Alaska, Hawaii, Puerto Rico. We dreamed, the sun hot on our faces, the smells of poplar trees and grass, and the thick, comforting stench of cow manure. We were tough and brassy and resilient, so sure we would get what we wanted that we pitied our mother and her doomed world of kitchen and mops and furniture polish.

That was when we were outside, where we were free to move and talk and walk, where no one watched or criticized or yelled about our elbows on the table, our dirty socks in the middle of the bathroom floor, our dolls and books lining the hallway. Our constant, shameful, tiring messes.

Inside, we became subdued and quiet. We walked on our toes, to make as little noise as possible. We spoke in soft voices, wiped our hands across our lips as if to erase our words. We became passive and crafty, watching and listening until we flew at each other and hit, punched, pulled hair. We were vicious, inflicting bruises and teeth marks over each other's arms and legs. We did this because we both understood, in that unspoken world of childhood, that such measures were critical and necessary, that every punch and pulled fistful of hair was a testimony to our bond, our kinship. That we did it as much out of love as anger.

⁓ ✸ ⁓

Back then, she was the favorite of my three sisters. Because we were the closest in age and because we lived on a farm, isolated from our nearest neighbor by more than a mile, we learned to curve ourselves around each other's behaviors. It's like a marriage, that kind of closeness, when you are together from morning until night, when you know someone so well that everything, from the way her breath smells in the afternoon to how fast her toenails grow, is familiar to you. It's beyond love, it has nothing to do with love. It's love in its purest, most basic form.

⁓ ✸ ⁓

How do I explain the humid landscape of my childhood, the anger and heated excitement, the ugly and awful silences?

There's something inhuman about a family living in a house together. All the misplaced passion and guilt, all the anger and unforgiven loss. We were, I suppose, like most families, better than some, worse than others.

I remember the evenings my two older sisters, my younger sister, and I packed together in the living room, in that small space without enough furniture, all four of us sitting on the floor, and we did so carefully, making sure not to touch one another. It would have been an agony to touch each other then, in the evenings when we all gathered together, watching TV or hiding behind books, our faces averted, the rustle of a page turning, the muffled interruption of a cough. We didn't look at one another, we rarely spoke, we were solitary, yet together as I sat there jealous and ashamed and hating those perfect television families.

⁓ჟᴄ⁓

Nights out in the country, nothing around for miles, no sound but the crickets and the trees rustling. Damp grass, and the sweet smell of hay. We wandered, Deena and I, for hours, until our mother's thin, high voice called us in. Deena's stockier legs running ahead. A flash of white T-shirt or maybe a barrette. In the pasture, where we were forbidden to go at night, we crept up behind the cows, seeking their warm animal comfort, their boring, bland breaths.

We liked to look at the stars, though we never learned their names. We felt no need to name them, the same way we felt no need to learn the names of the weeds we sucked on, instinctively avoiding those that were poisonous. We were safe outside in the fields and pastures, the dark expanses of hills and valleys shaped as soft and full as a woman's body. We nestled together, warm and quiet, slapping mosquitoes and digging our fingers into the cool and welcoming night ground.

Those were the years after our father died, when we lived on our stepfather's farm, ninety acres stretching out through woods and rolling hills, thick poplar trees and hidden valleys, where it was always cool and the mud was always moist, even during the hottest of days. The land was fecund and magical, it gave us blackberries and strawberries, crab apples sagging heavy on branches. All around, the heated sounds of growth, and beyond, the rustle of grasshoppers, the sway of the breeze, the snorts of the horses and mindless shuffling of cows.

I was eight when we moved out to the farm, Deena nine, Dawn ten, and Debbie, the baby, barely five. We were skinny and lost, little fatherless girls, though Deena was in fact chubby, but inside we were skinny and hungry and scared. We didn't understand what had happened or who these men were that we were suddenly living with, two stepbrothers and a stepfather. The brothers almost grown, one a football player with a kind heart and the only one who paid us much attention. He taught us how to catch a football and throw a basketball, gave us affectionate nicknames: I was the hippie, that's what he called me, hippie-girl because I hated to wear shoes, hated to comb my hair, loved drawing peace signs over my arms in magic marker.

The other stepbrother was strange and serious. We laughed at his jokes, though we didn't understand them. Probably, we weren't really listening.

My stepfather, though, what can I say about him? That he was brooding and moody, uncomfortable around people, especially women, especially children. He sat in the living room the nights he didn't work at the paper mill and ate Spanish peanuts or potato chips, chewing with his mouth half-opened, the noise of his teeth crunching until I covered my ears, humming to myself to get rid of those sounds. He didn't talk to us, never really talked to us. In the ten years I lived in that house, he never said happy birthday or merry Christmas, never got me a present or a card, never asked how I was, if I needed anything, if I was happy. If I gathered all the words he ever spoke to me, it wouldn't cover half of a notebook page.

He came from a true country background, hard times, a beaten-down house, and this shamed him. He read a lot, as if to make up for this, novels and magazines and the thick Bible he kept by his side of the bed. The only one he talked to was my mother, late at night in the living room, and later, when they got another TV, in their bedroom, his voice going on and on in the hick accent particular to where he had grown up.

My sisters and I were confused by this man who wasn't our father, who didn't act like a father, and we didn't understand why our mother insisted that we pretend that he was. But we did. We pretended that we were an ordinary family and that it was normal to have a father who ignored us, who never spoke to us, who rarely acknowledged us. We grew up pretending and became so good at it that it became part of our games, those wild-girl games we played out in the pastures, our faces flushed, our arms and legs covered with scratches and mosquito and spider bites.

"Pretend that didn't happen," we'd shout when we tripped or forgot to tag home base. "Pretend you didn't see me. Pretend I didn't fall. Pretend I didn't do that."

We played and fought, punched, and pulled hair, all the while pretending we were something we weren't. We couldn't help it. We wanted a storybook family, like in books and movies. We wanted a father who checked over our schoolwork and noticed when we came to the supper table with dirty hands. One who would praise us and punish us, and when that didn't happen, we learned to punish ourselves. All of us so hungry for a man's attention, we learned to take whatever crumbs we could find and lick them up. That little flush of pride: someone noticed me. We would grow up, all of us, to have problems with men, to be unable to find or keep love, to not understand the love of a man. Watching other women do this so easily, so casually, as we struggled and gasped. All the counselors and support groups, the medications for depression and anxiety and panic attacks. All of this when what we needed was simple: to have someone, anyone, sit us down and tell us, explain to us that, yes, we deserved a man's love.

Midsummer, fireflies flickering the edge of the fields, tiny sparks of color, persistent and magical, never-ending. My sisters and I running through the fields after dark, catching them in our hands and tucking them in glass jars, breathing holes punched through the top with nails. We placed these on our dressers, fell in and out of dreams as glows dotted across our bedroom walls. In the mornings, the fireflies were ordinary again, creeping around the bottom of the jars, sluggish and half-dead. We dumped them in the weeds beside the house, sure that as soon as dark hit, they'd light up once again. We were so hopeful, so certain. We loved catching those bugs, tiny flickers against our palms, the subtle flash of green giving our hands an unworldly glow. We felt blessed and immune, perfect lights tucked inside the captivity of our hands.

Legs long and tanned, gangling, moving with the unconscious gait of children, not realizing how soon grace would visit us.

He watched us. Woman-child, scrappy. We had no idea of our power, the things we would one day make men do.

He watched us, that is what I remember.

Him. Watching us.

We were forbidden to play in the old cars parked back in the woods, so of course we always did. Leather seats hot against our legs, smells of oil and dust and rotting plants. We fought over the best seats, we all wanted to drive, sit with our hands over the steering wheel, foot punching the gas and brake pedals. We rolled down the windows, stuck our elbows out, adjusted the mirrors. We played for hours, driving and talking of the places we would one day visit: California, Colorado, Florida.

The older cars, the uglier ones, we destroyed, pulling up the seats and slashing the upholstery with our stepbrother's pocket knife and then pulling out foam and cotton stuffing. We threw this around the woods, dancing and laughing, victorious with the power of destruction.

We killed bugs and spiders, smeared them over the back seats, blood and guts, and how we squealed and screamed, laughing and chasing each other with those dirty sticks.

Sometimes we discovered snakes curled up on the seats, sun-drenched and slow. We backed away, hushed, our hands over our mouths as if viewing a mystery. I jabbed one once on a dare, creeping up with a stick and touching it across its back, and when it raised its head, we yelled and clutched at each other. Its tongue flashed sly and smooth so that we wanted to kill it, hit it until it was a bloody mess, but it slipped away before we could catch it.

—◦—

Apple pie hot from the oven, that heavenly sugar burning our lips. My mother baked in the afternoons, when our stepfather was sleeping or working second shift. She was different then, warmer and softer when she was in the kitchen baking for us. We sat at the table, all four of us coloring and building things with clay and the slabs of rough wood we cut out in the garage. We were inventive and clever, we knew how to be quiet, though later we'd explode and hit, yell, slam doors, and throw things at each other. Not in the kitchen, though. Not while our mother was baking.

We liked the crust best, that dough that crumbled in our mouths, sprinkles of cinnamon tasting almost salty beyond the sweetness. We devoured this, always more comfortable with surfaces than the messy, thicker middles. When evening came, the crust would be gone, the pie naked except for the apples spilling out. My mother would yell and we'd hang our heads, apologize, swear we wouldn't do it again. We'd eat the sticky apples with milk for breakfast and it wouldn't even resemble a pie, nothing left but the filling, the part you don't normally see.

The next time my mother baked a pie, we'd do it again. We couldn't resist, it was too tempting, too extravagant, all that crust waiting for our fingers to pinch it off, place it in our mouths, claim it as our own.

Rainy days, Deena and I snuck over to the neighbor's house, where we were forbidden to play because they raised pigs and were classified as white trash. Their father a drunk, their mother fat and slow moving. We loved this farm, loved the mess and the stench, loved to hold the new piglets in our arms, the pressure of their mouths sucking our fingers. We snuck through the back field, cut across the side pasture, and crawled under the electric fence, our knees low to keep us from getting zapped. We were dirty by the time we knocked on the door, but no one cared. Bobby, who was in Deena's class at school, led us past the living room, where his mother spent the afternoons on the couch, empty bottles rolling over the filthy floor, his father outside yelling at the pigs. Dirty laundry piled over the stairs, plaster peeling, buckets placed over the floor to catch the rain leaking from the roof. Bobby had a chemistry set, and we spent long afternoons trying to fashion a bomb. We wanted to blow up the gravel pit, the crab tree in the far pasture, half dead from numerous lightning strikes. We drew up plans calculated to the tenth of an inch by Deena's mathematical mind while Bobby's father cursed at the pigs outside the window. On the way home, Deena and I whispered these words, laughing until we could barely speak: "Ass sucker. Cock creeper. Mother of all balls."

Saturday night we took baths, cleaned ourselves up, sat in church the next morning in our cotton dresses and patent leather shoes, impatient and hungry because we weren't allowed to eat before Mass, couldn't receive communion unless our bellies were empty and pure. Right before the Benediction, Deena leaned toward me, glasses slipping down her nose, her mouth so close I could feel the moisture on my ear as she whispered, teased, "Mother of all balls."

She was gutsy like that, back then.

We were working class poor. Everyone, almost, was poor. It was that type of place, farms and factory jobs, hand-me-downs, and if your boots had a hole in them, you stuffed newspaper and plastic bags inside and kept walking. Beside our church shoes, we had two other pairs. One was for play, cheap boy's sneakers bought on sale at the Kmart. Our school shoes were from a department store, a luxury. We felt out of place there. We could tell, from the way our mother hunched her shoulders and tightened her mouth, that we didn't belong. That we weren't good enough.

Deena and I curled next to each other, reading. We read fast, furiously; we read anything and everything we could get our hands on: romance books, comics, classics, magazines. We marked the pages and shared them later in our rooms, in the soft glow of the lamplight. We read out loud, our voices young and expressionless and proud. Sometimes we slept with our books, just to feel them next to us, that weight, that firm scratch of a rough binding. We cherished library books the most, because they were temporary, so we loved them with a mournful, childish love, knowing that we would soon have to give them up. It was the mystery that captured us, the not knowing whose hands had touched the pages, whose eyes had glanced over the words, the very same words we read late at night, a flashlight beneath our covers.

Once my oldest sister dropped a library copy of *Gone with the Wind* in the bathtub, the pages soaked, the binding withered and crunched. My mother was furious; we couldn't afford to replace it. We stuck it under the hair dryer and my mother ironed the worst of the pages, that fragile paper straightening as if by magic.

We were taught to care for things, books and words, but only if they were written. What we said didn't matter but what we wrote did. I don't know when I started to believe this, but it came to me early. By the time I was ten, I knew that I would be a writer. I knew this instinctively, unquestioningly.

Even then, I liked the people I read about in books more than those I knew in person.

Once a week, neighbor women stopped over for coffee cake, sitting at the wobbly Formica table without a tablecloth, drinking coffee or Lipton tea. Joking about men, talking about them as if they were children, one more person to pick up after, one more burden.

My mother wore the same hairstyle my entire childhood: cut short with the top bristled so that she could roll it up in plastic curlers after she washed it, inserting pink pins to hold everything in place. Horrible curlers with mean little spikes. When she took them off, she sprayed her hair with Aqua Net hairspray. It was a sensible style, no-nonsense, little fuss. Nothing soft or feminine, nothing that would make you want to reach out and touch it.

In the mornings, she exercised along with Jack LaLanne, scooting across the living room floor on her butt to keep it in shape because she didn't want to let herself go. She did toe touches and jumping jacks, the tail of her white blouse flying. My mother was tall and thin, with glasses too big for her face so that she always looked as if she were hiding behind those large ovals. She was afraid of getting fat, though she never came out and said it; still, we all knew that being fat was being weak, excessive, outlandish, and greedy, all the things we were taught not to be. I don't remember my mother ever overeating, ever sitting back from the supper table and cradling her stomach and saying, "Oh, I ate too much." I don't remember her looking forward to food, or closing her eyes and savoring the sugary piecrusts she made or the cakes or even the toughened gristle around the chicken wings she favored. She opened her mouth, she ate. This seemed to make her angry.

"If I don't eat, I'll be sick." As if food were something to keep your body fueled, a medicine. A chore, like bathing or brushing your teeth. She didn't fuss over meals. She cooked, put everything on the table, and we all sat down and ate. The food was never spicy or exotic, it was good country food. Heavy and nourishing. Meat and potatoes at every meal. Tall glasses of milk. Always dessert.

I don't know about Deena or my other sisters, but I looked forward to those meals, ran to the table, my eyes watering as I stared down at the mashed potatoes smothered in gravy, the green beans, the cucumber salad, the pork chops or Swiss steak or fried chicken. Stuffing it into my mouth as quickly as I could, barely chewing. I was always hungry. Often, I ate more than my stepbrothers, who were years older; one of them was a football player who weighed close to two hundred pounds. I never gained an ounce. I was skinny, scrawny, elbows and knees sticking out. It was impossible to find clothes that fit, and at school, the nurses sent notes home urging my mother to feed me more. These notes made her angry.

"They think I'm not feeding you," she said, her voice trembling. Insinuating that it was my fault, some type of stubbornness, as if I were willing my body to stay thin.

I ate and ate, that's what I remember of those years, the food, yes, but mostly the hunger.

~ ♋ ~

The horses down in the barn, grainy and smelling like musk, like sharp, angular heat. I spent as much time as I could around them, brushing and spreading hay, combing their necks, lifting their hooves and cleaning out the dirt with a pick, that sharp, cruel-looking hoof pick like a medieval instrument.

My favorite was a big, bay-colored gelding, almost seventeen hands, wild and unpredictable, kicking when I tried to put on the saddle, puffing his stomach as I tightened the cinch. Ears back, lips drawn, muscles tense: Don't fuck with me. I rode when he was like that, fighting to slip in the bit, tugging the bridle over his ear and then swinging onto his back, no saddle, just his hot, angry hide beneath my legs. Dangerous, the way we ran through the fields, no way of stopping or slowing down. My thighs tight, fists clutching the reins. Wind in my hair, strands of mane in my mouth until nothing mattered but the speed.

Often, I rode until my thighs bled beneath my thin shorts. A sweet, agonizing pain I later rubbed in bed, the intoxicating heat, the angry red lines. The next morning, I would be on that horse again, my legs chapped and aching. It was worth it, that pain, that blood. It was worth it to feel so free.

~ ♋ ~

I wanted him to die. I used to get down on my knees at night and pray that he would die, I didn't care how, a car accident or a heart attack. Something quick and final.

Deena must have prayed the same prayer, though we never mentioned this. It was too awful, too sinful. We wanted it too much.

⟿

Kool-Aid mixed with sugar and staining our lips. Bologna sandwiches slathered with Miracle Whip. Strawberry shortcake topped with the strawberries we picked back in the woods. In the summer, we poured Kool-Aid in Tupperware containers shaped like popsicles, sucked on them during the worst of the afternoon heat, sugar dripping our arms and legs. Sometimes our mother made cream puffs, dough fried warm, vanilla pudding inside and chocolate melted over the top, every bite so rich our stomachs ached but still we couldn't stop. My favorite dessert was lemon pie, the meringue beaten until it was light and fluffy. I loved the tang of lemon, the tartness filling my tongue, followed by the soft dream of meringue. My mother didn't make this often, since it was hard work, so it was more of a treat. A luxury, she called it. For years whenever I saw rich people on television, I imagined my mother in their kitchens baking lemon meringue pies.

⟿

I was not a pretty child, my hair thin and sticking to my face, my arms and legs skinny, knees and elbows jutting out. Eyes blue and always watching. I didn't like to talk, didn't understand the concept of language, all those words stringing together, and when those around me spoke, I closed my eyes and rocked back and forth, thinking of the telephone wires along the highway when we rode into the city, how they went on and on; they never seemed to end. That's how I felt when people talked. I became lost, tangled, and grownups were forever scolding me, yelling at me to listen, please listen, didn't I hear a word they said?

I never felt comfortable around people, crowds of people, or even groups. In school, I was popular, I worked hard at this, I knew it was important in some wordless way, yet what relief arriving home and running out in the fields with Deena, both of us silent as we slapped mosquitoes and tossed rocks in the creek.

Riding bikes, crawling through drainage pipes, catching tadpoles and daddy longlegs and grasshoppers. I put everything in my mouth, tasted everything: rusty nails, old bottle caps, the sloped, pulsing heads of frogs. My tongue sticking out tentatively, and then touching, tasting.

It was, I suppose, the way I spoke. My own secret language.

Gramma, my mother's mother, was a proper lady. Always pressed and neat, clothes matching, fake pearls around her neck, clip-on earrings that turned her earlobes a bright red. She fed us soft-boiled eggs and orange juice with so much water it was almost tasteless. She was afraid of excesses and bright colors and any type of passion. Her life was orderly and frail, based on routine.

Her neck so thin, her hair colored blue at the beauty parlor once a month. Her husband had been an alcoholic, though she would never admit it, never utter the word. After he died, she didn't date or remarry. It was as if she was a husk, so removed from her body that it became something to wash and pat with powder and hang clothes on. An obligation, a chore.

After church, we stopped by her apartment in the city, my mother warning us to be good as we ran, all four of us, up those steps, our Mary Janes slipping on the polished wood.

Knocking at the door, barging in. We were wild country girls, used to wide-open spaces and loud noises. We raced through the living room, hopping on the flowered rug, knocking over lamps and scattering pillows. Laughing, fighting, crying. We always ended up in our grandmother's bedroom, rummaging through her jewelry box, those gaudy beads, those brooches as big as our palms. Dressing up, parading around while our grandmother sat in her chair, smiling and clapping.

Each one of us knew, was sure that we were the one that she loved the best.

I wanted to escape, that's what I longed for, what we all longed for, my sisters and I. Reinforced with every book we read, every movie we saw, our eyes intent, our bodies silent and watchful, as if waiting for a clue, a sign, something that would let us know how to do this thing we wanted so badly, that we craved and feared and cried about, late at night, our pillows hot and twisted with our angry, heated yearnings.

Most of the women wanted to leave. No matter how much they said they loved the land, the farms, the quiet, hazy mornings. No matter how much they said these things, how much they meant them, truly meant them, they still wanted to leave, wished to leave, were jealous and spiteful when someone did this, when a woman left, escaped. That most stayed put, surrounded by lives they could trace like the back of their hands, didn't faze us.

We were smart, and sly. We were different, more isolated, more desperate. It wasn't if we would get away. It was when. Throughout our childhood, we rehearsed it over and over: waiting to leave, getting ready to leave. It's something I'm still good at, that one shining moment when I pack up and leave.

My mother made our lunches for school. We couldn't afford to buy lunches and my mother was ashamed of the red discs they handed out for the poorer kids. Each night she packed our lunches, wrapping sandwiches and slices of cake in waxed paper and carefully placing them in brown bags with our names written across in pencil.

I loved those lunches. I loved the grade school cafeteria and how it smelled of canned peas and sweaty feet and old meat. I loved the long tables and the way we swung our legs over the benches to sit down.

My favorite sandwich was Cheez Whiz with relish, that tang of sour pickles against the richness of the imitation cheese. Other days it was meatloaf sandwiches thick with ketchup, bologna and mustard, tuna salad with chopped celery, peanut butter and jelly. The only thing I hated was Underwood Deviled Ham and this I choked down, my eyes watering, my throat tight as I tried to swallow without tasting. I don't know why I didn't throw it away, but I never did. I suppose it never occurred to me.

The secrets in that house at night, the sound of feet padding up the hallway. Lying in bed, covers pulled up to my chin. Not moving, not even breathing. Counting the steps: five, six, seven. Please, God, no. The shadow of an arm, the glow of a cigarette. The footsteps moving away, down the hall to Deena's room. The soft sounds of her voice protesting. I pulled a pillow over my head, recited the alphabet, the multiplication tables, the names of all the explorers. Barely breathing, waiting for it to be over.

In the morning, we never spoke of the things that happened at night, in that house. In the soft overhead light of the breakfast table, our mother fixed us eggs and toast. She fixed hot breakfasts, she believed in nourishing our stomachs before school, she believed in education, in books and reading. She wanted us to have a different life, to get away. We ate, warmth coating our throats, and in that kitchen, we truly believed that those other things, those nighttime things, didn't exist. We pushed them to the backs of our minds as we crunched bread crusts, added milk to oatmeal, cut our forks through the syrupy goodness of French toast. We wiped our mouths, brushed our teeth, stepped outside into the damp country air, fields stretching out in all directions as we waited for the school bus to pull up to the driveway, open its door, take us away.

This is a lie, all of this. It's not the way it really happened.

Maybe for Deena, but not for me.

Or maybe it was. Maybe this is all true, every word, every line.

Maybe I just want to pretend that it isn't.

I have to tell you this: There were times when the sun shone and my hair was wet and the world was good. Days when I popped the tops off dandelions and chewed them with my strong teeth, swallowed that yellow sweetness. Nights when I crawled through the grass, just to feel the dampness against my knees.

I knew things, then. How to strip a branch until the milky whiteness swam into view. How to burrow through the mud in the creek and catch crayfish in my hands. How to sit so still in the woods a deer would push its velvet nose in the leaves beside my feet.

Even the dirt was a pleasure, and often I picked it up, held it to my nose, welcoming the sweet, loamy odor of rot.

Corn fritters fried in butter and topped with maple syrup, so sickeningly sweet that we couldn't stop eating. Cucumbers fresh from the garden, the skins warm from the sun. Swiss steak on Wednesdays, tuna casserole or salmon loaf on Fridays, because we were Catholic and didn't eat meat on Fridays.

Sundays we went to church, driving all the way over to the next town, the windows rolled up even in the heat of summer so that we wouldn't mess our hair. I sat between Deena and Debbie in those hard pews, moving my mouth during the songs because I didn't like singing in church, hated the way voices echoed from the tall ceiling. Deena folded her program into shapes, itched mosquito bites, chewed her lip. We all stood for Communion, though Debbie was too young to receive. Walking up the aisle, kneeling down.

"The body of Christ." The old priest holding out the wafer.

"Amen." Our mouths and bellies pure. We weren't allowed to eat before church, not if we wanted Communion, and our stomachs grumbled; even that dry disc of flavorless bread was welcomed. We held it in our mouths, tucked it against our cheeks, tried to make it last.

When our grandmother had extra money, we stopped at Stuckey's on the way home for cinnamon rolls, fat pastries thick with nuts. Fingers sticky, dresses smeared. Taking small bites so that it would last longer. Windows opened now, breeze in our hair. We closed our eyes, pinched each other's legs. We played a game where we dug our fingernails into one another's arms, harder and harder, until we cried, "Uncle." We were fierce and tough; we hated to lose. Half-moon scratches up and down our arms, drops of blood over the back seat. We licked our arms clean, savoring the salt blood.

"Say uncle," we taunted, pressing our nails deeper into one another's arms, nails ripping skin.

I held off until the pain burned and tightened, until it sharpened into a word, a vowel, a color, tight and hard and high.

Forehead scrunched, eyes tightening, breath held taut; I held off until finally I had to say it, had to whisper, "Uncle."

When the pain stopped, I almost missed it.

—⁓—

What can I say about my mother all those years? She was such a big part of the picture yet stayed in the background, where she was most comfortable. She was nervous, unsure. She wore stretch pants with stirrups, sweatshirts, her hair short and no-nonsense. She never asked much of herself so she didn't ask much of us.

We knew, early on, that we couldn't count on her, that she wasn't strong enough to hold us up. She was weak, and to me and my sisters, country girls with tough country attitudes, this was the worst of her sins, not that she didn't see or hear or acknowledge but that she was scared. We didn't know what she was scared of, we only knew that we couldn't count on her. She supplied the food and cleaned the house and bought us school clothes and made sure we did our homework and took us to the library and church and baked cupcakes for school functions, but we never told her other things, deeper things, the important things. We didn't share our dreams or desires, the things that frightened us, our anxieties or troubles.

"Don't tell Ma," we said, and we said this early on. When we had a bad time in school, when we needed a teacher's note signed because of bad behavior, we sought one another, we forged notes and permission slips, we comforted and scolded. In high school when I went out on dates, it was Dawn, my oldest sister, who waited up, not my mother, and once, when I came home late, my clothes messed from some boy's hot kisses, it was Dawn who yelled and slapped my face and ordered me to my room.

My mother didn't reveal much of her life and what little she told us was unhappy: stories of her overprotective mother,

of how she threw up before her first date with our father. She
often threw up in these stories, she threw up from nervousness or stress or fear. Her stomach was often upset. She didn't
seem happy.

She was physically strong, though. She walked and rode a
bike over the country roads. She stacked hay in the barn and
helped with the cows. Once, when we were the only ones home
and a laboring cow was in trouble, the two of us pulled out
the dead calf with a rope, we slung it around those two tiny
and precious hooves sticking out from the cow and then we
pulled, we stood in that hot, stuffy barn, in cow manure up to
our ankles, with a cow half dead from pain and exhaustion, and
we pulled and cried, pulled and swore, until finally that calf slid
out. It was dead and perfectly formed, its eyes opened, its legs
bent at an angle, as if ready to run. The smell was hideous, rotten and sharp and cutting, as if that calf had to make up for its
too-short life and could do so only through smell. We carried
it out to the manure pile behind the barn, set it down gently,
shoveled dirt until it was buried. We were filthy and sweating
and covered with blood, and neither of us could stop crying,
but we did it. We birthed and then buried that calf.

So I suppose my mother has always been a strong woman,
just not strong in the way we needed.

I was afraid to sing when I was a child. I was sure my voice
was hideous, dreadful. Of course, that's a lie. I sang the way all
children sing, in a loud, cheerful voice, a voice of vast spaces
and hidden rooms. A voice that promised to take me where I
wanted to go.

I can't remember Deena singing, isn't that something? I
can't remember one song she sang, though she must have. In
church, right next to me, and still I can't remember her, I can't
remember any of them: my mother, grandmother, my sisters.

Only my own voice rising loud and joyously off-key: "Holy, holy, holy . . ."

As if God could hear. As if he were fucking listening.

—∿—

There were places in the woods where the ground was littered with pine needles and moss, the air soft with no sound; even my footsteps were silent. Pine trees hanging overhead, the shade cool and dank. A hawk lived back there, gliding through the sky with large, harsh wings. Lying on my back and watching it fly, I felt the pulse of my throat humming, but no sound. Quiet. Still. The horse off grazing somewhere, the dog sniffing around the raspberry bushes. Some days I stayed like that for hours, not reading or thinking, just lying in the grass and looking up at the sky.

—∿—

Every summer, we visited the zoo. We piled in the car and drove the long, hot way in to the city. We took a lunch and ate in the picnic area, ham sandwiches squished between waxed paper, the mustard warm and tangy. Bottles of Dad's root beer and cream soda. Greasy potato chips. It was a feast, sitting at those worn tables, initials carved over the top, words we didn't yet understand: fuck, cunt, bitch. The smell of hot animals and urine-soaked straw drifting over us.

We argued over who got what flavor of pop, the best sandwiches, the biggest handful of chips. Legs mosquito-bitten in shorts, cheap Kmart sneakers, shirts already smeared with ketchup and potato salad. Our bad haircuts, our sneaky, furtive glances, the way we bared our teeth when we bit into our sandwiches. We felt out of place in the city, surrounded by other kids with more money and better clothes. We were loud amongst ourselves but quiet when others came up. Hesitant; almost shy.

One of us always cried when we got to the zoo. All those animals locked up in cages, that hopeless mood of defeat. I liked the gorilla best, a doomed, black hulk of fur with a human face. I'd stand in front of its cage, a glass partition between us, and will it to look at me, look me in the eye, but it never did.

~~~

The pond in the summer. Mosquitos lazy from the heat. Flies droning. The four of us in swimsuits, skin tanned, faces flushed from the sun. Jumping off the diving board, clasping our knees between our arms. Cannonball, we called it. Seeing who could jump the farthest, stay under the longest.

The pond smelled like cows, even though it was enclosed in a fence. Still, the creek that fed into it was the same one used by the cows, and sometimes pieces of dried dung floated by, usually in the shallow end, where the reeds grew rich and tall in the heat. We didn't care. We loved that water, dark and cold and dangerous. We swam for hours, we hated to come out.

Our mother sat in a lawn chair up on the bank, reading magazines and novels. She read while we swam, and as we became older, she stayed at home and we watched each other.

Once I saved my little sister Debbie, pulled her up from where she was struggling under the water after wading out too deep, her thin arms trying to pump, her legs useless and scared. I grabbed her by the hair, yanked her up. Her face pale, mouth spitting up water. I leaned her over the diving board, whacked her too hard on the back. I was angry, furious with fear.

"Weakling," I whispered, leaning down until her cold ear touched my mouth. "Little show-off, little coward. Trying to go out too far."

I was so angry that I cried, we both cried, I leaned over, slapped her on the back, crying, screaming.

"Too far. Why did you have to go out so far?"

He never touched her. Never a wrong look, a watchful eye; we wouldn't have allowed it. Not her. The youngest.

I don't know why or how we came up with this. Whether it was instinct or something else, something that carried in our blood, some sense of family loyalty. Or maybe it simply had to do with love.

But he never touched her. That's one thing. She's never had to be afraid of a bed, sheets, the pressed smell of a pillowcase waiting for someone else's head. She grew up without that fear, that ugliness.

We did this one thing.

Holy thing.

Kind thing.

God-awful fucking good thing.

I remember the summer the farm flooded, one of those August storms, so fierce and sudden it was like anger or temptation. Like a sin, that's how the flood felt, cool and quick and over-powering, like a sin I was waiting to commit.

The pastures ran with water until it was up past my knees. We herded the horses and cows to higher ground and then my sisters and I ran through that water, we ran and splashed in the old shorts and shabby tennis shoes our mother insisted we wear because "no one knew what was under all that water."

I kicked mine off, watched the current carry them away, those old, blue, boy's shoes, flat soled and cheap, the laces always untying, the toes curled upward from too many hours in the creek. My feet bare in that moving water, small rocks, sticks, the pinch of an old piece of farm machinery. I ran wild, intoxicated from the water and the cold flush against my skin where it touched me. I took off my shirt, threw it down in that water, laughing, rain falling on my bare shoulders. I slipped out of my shorts, and then my underpants, naked except for the water. Dunking my head under and then standing up, laughing, screaming.

That cold rain. My hot, hot blood.

~ ✤ ~

Deena believed in God. It was inconceivable that she could do that, believe in something so nebulous and indistinct. That she could have faith, blind faith, and let herself believe in those lies and demands. All those years of church, those Monday night catechism classes at the fire hall, the instructors a married couple with over a dozen children. They were poor, they had bad teeth, dirty hair, the girls in old rummage sale clothes, walking with that leaning-over walk of a girl brought up to be ashamed of her breasts.

We sat in those classes, smug and defiant. Or at least I thought we did, though maybe it was just me. All those lessons and crayon-filled sheets where we colored the heavens, the seas, the loaves of bread and fish. I nodded my head, memorizing passages, lifting my voice and singing with the rest of the group. But I couldn't understand the idea of faith or why I was being forced to believe something I couldn't see or feel or taste. It was beyond my comprehension; I couldn't grasp the reality of it.

But Deena must not have seen it that way. She must have allowed herself to believe, small kernels seeping through her ears and eyes. She was good at memorizing, she got the highest marks on tests and quizzes, could recite passages without a quiver. I thought it was all for show, but maybe it wasn't. Maybe even then she believed, wanted to believe, needed to believe.

Maybe she needed something no one else could give her.

~ ✤ ~

Once Deena and I swam in the pond at night, in that vast country darkness, the moon washing everything in a pale light that was filmy and pure. The water warm on our cold skin, and the way it felt as we dived in, pulling us down toward the thick mud on the bottom. Lying on our backs and stroking across the width of the pond, our bodies offered up unashamedly to the night sky. A flicker of stars, a slight breeze over our nipples. Moving through that water for hours, until we were afraid we might fall asleep and sink down forever.

That's a lie, it wasn't both of us, only me, alone in the moonlight with my pale, new breasts. But she should have been with me, in that darkness, that water, that silver-streaked light. She should have been there.

———

Don't speak, he warned, hand clamped over my mouth. Don't say a word. Breath hot on my neck, hand tasting of salt and vinegar. I never spoke, never uttered a sound, I was so good, such a nice girl. So thin and trusting and nice. So clean. Afterward I scrubbed myself in the bathroom, a washcloth between my legs until I was almost raw. My eyes watering, my teeth biting my lips: it was the only way I could make myself cry.

———

Strawberries back in the woods, sweet and tangy. Raspberries in the corner by the dump, smearing juice down our arms and legs. Crab apple trees along the edge of the front pasture, small and bitter, we ate them until our stomachs ached and still we couldn't stop. Sweet grass, clover, dandelions, morning glories, black-eyed Susans, Indian paintbrush, and a plant we called salt and pepper. The air heavy with smells and sounds and tastes. So much abundance, how could it be possible that we were always so hungry?

This is what I like to remember, the long Memorial Day weekends and how we kept track of the countdown on the radio station, all of us sitting cross-legged in the bedroom, slurping cereal and frantically writing down the titles. We were anxious, doing this, that we might miss one. We wrote on lined paper, our handwriting getting messier and messier as the morning went on. By afternoon, we were out lying in the yard on blankets, the radio turned up high enough that we could hear it over our occasional bickering.

We tried to guess the number one song. It was usually something popular that summer, and we placed bets on which one it would be. I don't remember if I was ever right, or what or if I ever won. What I remember is the way we all were together, on that day we honored the dead, listening to music and writing down the names, almost as if the real world, the outside world, didn't exist beyond the boundaries of our farm.

Late in the afternoon, we went to the cemetery to clear our father's grave. We followed my mother and grandmother, we carried flowers we bought near the cemetery gates, my grandmother and mother arguing over how expensive they were, but it was essential to have flowers, fresh flowers. My mother and grandmother kneeling in front of the graves with their clippers and gloves and vases, the things needed to keep the graves looking neat. It was important that the graves be maintained, that other people, when walking through the cemetery, knew that someone cared, that these people, my father and grandfather, and beyond them, other, lesser relatives, were once loved. That they once had a life.

My sisters and I took off through the rolling hills of the cemetery, racing back and forth, jumping over the graves, yelling and shouting, hair flying, tanned arms pumping back and forth. We were happy in that cemetery, close enough to our father to feel safe yet removed enough from his memory that we didn't feel grief. Our favorite game was skipping from one stone to the next, careful of not stepping on any grass. I was best at this, with my long legs and thin, flat feet. I'd kick off my shoes and, holding them in my fist, stretch my legs, hold my breath, and jump. That's what I still think of when I think of that cemetery: Jumping. My legs moving. And that sudden, exhilarating thud when my feet landed firmly on the stones of Irish and Italian and Polish names.

Our grandmother yelled when she saw us jumping on the stones, she felt we were disrespecting the dead, but for once our mother took our side.

"Leave them alone, Mother," she would say, her voice thick as steel as she pulled grass from around our father's grave. "They're kids. Let them be."

Our grandmother always showed us the plot waiting, right next to our grandfather, for her when she died: "This is where I will be." My sisters and I nodded solemnly, but really, we didn't care. We were young and strong; death was the furthest thing from our minds, especially in the sunlight, with the smell of grass and the air cool and wet from the lake, just minutes away.

Did we ever think, did we ever know, was there any sign, during those long summer days at the cemetery, that my Deena would be the next to go, after our grandmother? Did she ever slip on a grave, cut herself, her blood anointing that sacred, holy ground? Did she know, did anyone ever know, was there any sort of warning? Or were we really that blind and deaf, four girls with dirty fingernails and scraped knees running through the cemetery without a care in the world?

Were we ever, is it possible; were we ever that innocent, that unaffected, that goddamned beautiful?

INTERLUDE 1

Anchorage, Alaska

Sometimes I'll forget. I'll see a sweater while shopping or remember a line from a book I read as a child and I'll think: I have to tell Deena. Sometimes I even pick up the phone but stop midway to my ear, the phone hanging in the air like a hesitation, or a doubt.

Summer nights I walk the dog along the beach, salt smells and cloudy skies, the water stretching out in silver motion. I kick off my shoes, the sand cool and moist. About a half mile up, right before the marsh begins, there's a spot where the sand is white and soft. I lean against a water-bleached log, stare out at the water, the movement soothing and hypnotic.

When the tide comes in, I walk to the shoreline, waves crashing my feet and then pulling back with a force that reminds me of labor pains, how my body contracted and opened, contracted and opened. The water is female, the tide a midwife. I stay in that cold water until it creeps past my knees, teasing my thighs, and it's difficult, so difficult, to leave, to call the dog and walk back to the trailhead and the car and my ordinary and nondescript life.

I'm happiest, always, when outdoors.

Those first years I set out food for Deena on her birthday and on the anniversary of her death. I don't know what she ate toward the end, probably what she ate for years, white foods, bland and forgiving, all color and flavor bleached from the surface. I set crackers and oatmeal and a small packet of protein powder on a plate and placed it in the middle of the table. Once,

I lit a candle, though it didn't seem right. The mood was too somber, too oppressive, and finally I blew it out.

A few months later, while hiking in the mountains with my son, we came across bear tracks on the trail, large prints; they must have belonged to a grizzly. My son placed both feet inside the print, and we marveled. The prints were fresh but not recent, probably a few days old, maybe a week.

"Should we go on?" I asked. I didn't want him to be scared, but I didn't want him to turn away from his fears, either.

He shrugged his small shoulders. "Dying from a bear would be better than a car accident or murder."

"Probably," I said, "though I doubt we'll die."

"Still, it would be better," he insisted. "There wouldn't be anger or hate."

I wanted to hug him but he was at that age where he was beginning to shrug off hugs. I let go of the dog's collar and we continued hiking in the same direction, the air cool and, all around us, the deep and forgiving greens of summer.

On a late summer evening, I burn the pages from my sister's notebook. I do this on the beach, alone in the blurry lavender twilight, and quickly, because the tide is coming in and I don't want to be caught on the bluffs.

I don't know why I'm burning my sister's words, one of the few things I have left of her, along with her ID, a blue comb, a few photo albums, and a couple of hair ties that I sometimes wear around my wrist. Yet it seems necessary. She's been gone for almost a decade. A few nights before, I dreamed of her, angry and persistent—she wanted something I couldn't give.

When I woke, I decided to set her words free. Her notebook isn't happy, I don't know if it's a journal or fiction; it appears to be both. Reading it over, a story line emerges, a woman and a man, the usual heartbreak, the usual cries of betrayal, of wanting both revenge and to lie down and just fucking die. What woman hasn't lived that story? Yet hidden inside is another story, my sister's story, and I read it carefully, trying to make sense of her thoughts, decipher her word choices, the rhythm of her sentences. All the literature courses I took in college, all the analyzing, the studying. How odd that it should bring me here to this moment, kneeling in the sand on a small beach in Alaska in front of a fire slowly coaxed from damp driftwood, feeding small slips of my sister's notebook to the flame, her voice rising up like the phoenix.

I have no myrrh to offer, no egg, just the gift of my hands feeding stingy scraps of paper into the fire.

PURGING

Words from the Dead

It's the funny thing about being in trouble. You are the last one to see the connections.

—from Deena's notebooks

Northwestern Pennsylvania

There's a picture of Deena hanging above my desk, thumb-tacked to the wall, bare and unadorned. I can't stand the idea of hiding her face behind glass, locking her within the boundaries of a frame. I like the fact of her photograph hanging free, the edges waving in the breeze when I open the windows.

The picture is from the earlier years, before she started throwing up and starving herself, when her face was still round and full. She's wearing glasses, cat-eyed brown frames, and her hair is parted to the side with a large piece slanting over her forehead. We all wore our hair that way, then. She must have been in sixth, maybe seventh grade. When we were still young.

I stole this picture when I was back home for the funeral. Late at night while everyone was sleeping, I pulled the photo albums out of the hall closet and went through each one. I don't know what I was looking for: a hint, a clue. I wanted to document just when it all went bad, but of course that was impossible. It's easy to lie in a photograph: a smile, a clean shirt, a lake shining behind you. From a distance, it's easy to look happy, play the part. We were good at doing that.

I took this picture because I thought it was during the last of the happy times, those summers we roamed the fields with the cows and horses, those last few years of thinking that the world would embrace us. But looking at it now, I see that it's false. We weren't happy then, she isn't happy. I can see that now. The way her smile tightens around the corners of her mouth. The dark circles beneath her eyes. It must have been happening to her then, the nighttime footsteps, and the way we both crouched in our sleep, ready to spring up and defend ourselves.

Though of course we never did. But still, in this picture, she was young, she hadn't given up yet. She still thought she would make it. I suppose she was defending herself, just in a different sort of way.

She's wearing a red sweater, her hair shining and soft. That's what I like to think when I look at the picture. That there was a time when she lifted her head and looked directly into a camera, when she wasn't afraid of being fully seen.

～ॐ～

By the time I was thirteen, I hated myself. Hated my skinny legs and lanky hair, my awful girl's body that wasn't as fast or tough or hard as a boy's. My thin, sharp face, my mouth that felt soft and bruised, like a rotting piece of fruit. I was afraid of my words, even then, of what they might say. I never knew what might come out of my throat.

There was a girl in my class, a poor girl. We were all poor, in one sense or another, but some families were more so, and these were the only ones we called poor. This girl was heavy and slow, ponderous, her breasts already starting to form by fourth grade. Her knees crusted with gray dirt, her socks drooping around her ankles. She wore skirts too big for her, handed down from one of her sisters, the waistband rolled up so that the uneven hem swished against her legs when she walked.

I recognized something of myself inside this girl, though I was years away from understanding how much alike we were, how we were both stubborn and unresisting, refusing to conform, intent on doing our own thing, going our own way. She didn't have many friends, played by herself at recess. I longed to huddle with her dirty hands and old sweater and the way she smelled in the winter from their coal stove. I wanted to find out what she dreamed of, where she went during class when her eyes drooped and her mouth opened, the tip of her tongue pressed against the corner of her lips.

I never did, though. I kept with my own friends, from the better families, neat and clean every morning, but during recess we went wild, threw dirt and stones, splashed in the mud, ran and pushed until we were dirty and gasping, our hair strangled around our faces. Often we picked on this other girl, in those vicious tormenting tones of children, we taunted, yelled insults, threw pebbles at her back and laughed when she flinched. We were wild and unrelenting, safe within our group.

I don't know what happened to this girl. The family moved away before we reached high school. Sometimes I imagine calling her up, hearing her breath rasp on the other end. "I'm sorry," I'd say. I don't know why I feel a need to apologize, if it's for me or her or both of us, the girls we once were, the women we've now become.

In this fantasy she doesn't say anything, she never answers. Still, I hold the receiver tight to my ear, waiting.

We cut ourselves, Deena and I. Never together, and we never talked about it. I don't know who did it first. Me, I think, though she would probably have said the same thing. The razor cool and sharp. It was a blessing, to feel that pain, my flesh tearing, a moment of silence, of nothing happening. And then the blood coming, slowly at first, and then more and more.

I stayed away from my veins. I didn't want to die. I wanted to hurt, to bleed. I wanted to shed the anger and pain, all those sounds locked inside my veins. I was always surprised at the color of my blood: red and bright, like anyone else's. I expected it to be black and thick, with that heavy, sweet odor of rot.

Summer evenings, I rode with my mother and Deena to the old fire hall where they held weekly dances. Local bands blared while we shook our hips and flipped our hair back and forth, trying to catch the attention of the boys, who stood against the wall, smoking and sneaking sips of the whiskey they kept in their pockets. Deena and I were at the stage where we hated each other, we embarrassed each other. We didn't speak the whole ride, and once we got out of the car, we walked in together, because we knew our mother was watching, and then we quickly parted. I was fourteen, tanned, my hair bleached with Sun In. I wore little tops tied up under my breasts, my belly flat and bare, my jeans so low on my hips I couldn't wear underpants. All my friends dressed this way. We stood around and drank whiskey or scotch we smuggled from our parents' cupboards. We took pills: Tylenol, Excedrin, Midol. We bought red-coated capsules one of the girls stole from her mother's prescription painkillers. We swallowed these down with beer or wine or whiskey and waited for our heads to fly. Then we stepped out on the dance floor and moved until we were wet with sweat. We forgot about trying to impress the boys, we forgot about how we looked, all the hours we spent picking our outfits and fixing our hair. We forgot everything except the beat of the music in our veins, the way the drums throbbed up from the wooden floor and hit us right between the legs. We didn't understand about sex, not yet, but we understood about longing, about wanting.

During intermission I snuck off with boys out in their cars. We all did this, if we were lucky enough to capture someone's attention. I snuck off in cars with bad mufflers and even worse paint jobs, cars that smelled of cigarette smoke and beer, cars with fuzzy dice hanging from the rearview mirror and imitation sheepskin seat covers in the back seat, and I struggled with whatever boy I happened to be with. We kissed, stuck our tongues deep into each other's mouths. We ran our hands up and down the bare skin of each other's arms, bellies, chests. We moaned, panted, whispered things we didn't mean. I took off my shirt, arched my back to the feel of some boy's tongue around my breasts.

We always stopped there. It was an unspoken code, something we just knew, and finally the boy (whose name I rarely bothered to learn, who always went to a different school, who usually wore a letter jacket and had another girl's ring around his neck) retied my shirt and we drank more before stepping back into the dance, separately, as if not to call attention to ourselves.

When I got home, I sat alone in my dark bedroom and cut my arms with a razor blade, one cut for each boy, as if trying to keep score.

I lie, I've always lied. Growing up, we all lied, though perhaps this is common in most families, the ability and need to lie. I lied, we lied, and it didn't matter what the lie was: a comment, a threat, a betrayal of one sort or another. What mattered was that we said it, did it, expanded our version of the truth until it was stretched and tarnished, pulled so far out of shape no one would recognize it.

We were sly, especially Deena and I, unlucky middle children. We lied and struggled and then, during the calm parts, out in the pasture or down in the basement, we re-created what had really happened, adding and subtracting until it better fit our skins and smells and awful, heated energies.

If anyone had asked, we each would have sworn that our version was true, having pushed what had really happened so deep in our minds that it was erased, smeared over, like the dead caterpillars we rubbed over rocks, saving the colors and then brushing them over our arms, yellows and browns and, when we were lucky, brilliant orange. Coloring ourselves a new past, a better version, like a book we might read and, not liking the ending, rip out pages from and rewrite to better suit our mood. We were clever and smart, intent upon survival. The truth wasn't important, we didn't give one damn about the truth. It was our lies that mattered. Our wonderful, terrible, god-beautiful lies.

Late summers, we helped bring in the hay, all of us dressed in old pants and long-sleeved blouses, gardening gloves on our hands. Deena drove the tractor, a coveted job, while the rest of us trudged through the fields, picking up the hay shooting off the baler. That's what we did for hours, for days, until we fell into a rhythm: bend, lift, heft with a knee and throw the bales up on the hay wagon, where my mother stacked them into neat piles. Sun hot so that sweat ran down our faces, hayseed in our hair and eyes and mouths, scratches over our necks and legs, cuts across our palms from the baling twine. At the end of the day, we headed into the house, where my mother had dinner warming in the oven, and we all sat down to chicken and mashed potatoes, biscuits thick with margarine, green beans fresh from the garden. No one talking, the sounds of chewing and swallowing. We ate as if we were starving, as if it was our last meal. My mother's biscuits were soft and doughy, with an odd aftertaste that I cherished. I couldn't get enough. I ate five, six, seven. Table manners forgotten, because it was haying season and we were allowed this one luxury, to eat without adornment, to reach and grab, to chew and swallow with greed and selfishness. We were united, then, my sisters and I, we sat at the table and ate with a purity, an animal contentment, that I still long for, still envy.

For years I hid food in my room, Jolly Rancher candies, the green ones, and crackers and cookies, sometimes apples that rotted and filled the room with a sweet, autumn smell. Pieces of bread from supper, fat slices of Velveeta cheese, a sandwich leftover from lunch. I didn't eat this food, I wrapped it in cellophane and tucked it in my dresser drawer, beneath my underpants and socks. When it became moldy, I threw it out and began collecting more. I don't know why I did this. It wasn't that I was hungry, it was more that I needed it. I didn't feel as lonely, knowing that food was within reach.

—◦—

By the time she reached high school, Deena had turned bad. That's what everyone said, everyone agreed: she was bad. After she was caught shoplifting, there was talk of reform schools, foster programs.

"Let them take me!" she cried. "I hate it here, hate everyone, I hate you all."

A few weeks later, she punched her arm through the front door window. It was a hot day, the air unmoving, all of us tense and angry, the heat pressing down until we could barely breathe. Sitting around the table at lunch, picking at our food because it was too hot to eat, too goddamned hot to do anything.

Then a shout, high pitched, like a warrior charging into battle, and Deena ran past, her arm held high above her head as she made straight for the door. The shatter of glass, Deena's fist punched through the window. Blood trickling over the floor, Deena holding out her arm, slivers of glass gleaming like knives.

I wish I could say that we ran over, helped bandage up her arm, checked to make sure that she was okay. But we sat paralyzed, no one making a sound. Finally, Deena stomped off to the bathroom, spots of blood dripping over the carpet. She cleaned her arm by herself while the rest of us sat at that table, that doomed, heated table. We sat there unmoving, as if stuck, or held fast.

—◦—

I no longer roamed the fields or ran barefoot through damp grass. My recklessness was gone, and so was my abandon.

I rarely rode the horses and they were eventually sold off, and each time I cried, I wept for hours, sitting in their empty stalls, my T-shirt tight against my face as I punished myself for having not loved them more. And slowly I stopped doing everything I loved. I spoke as little as possible, I stopped eating at mealtimes, sneaking into the kitchen late at night and shoving food into my mouth, whatever I could find: cold chicken and white bread, slices of processed cheese and overripe bananas. I quit washing my hair and bathed only when I had to.

My mother finally took me to the doctor, a country doctor the next township over. We walked inside his office with the creaky floor and a small, stuffy waiting room, the radio droning on in the background, and he asked how I was sleeping. I didn't answer. I sat in my old T-shirt, my shorts rolled up because they were now too big, my arms so thin, my collarbone sticking up like something unprotected. He prescribed sedatives, but I never took the pills. I didn't want to sleep. I wanted to stay awake, my eyes opened. I wanted to see everything but feel nothing. I started cutting myself in earnest, moving from my arms to my legs, carving words into my skin: *Me. No. Help.* Sometimes I wrapped bandages around these cuts, sat at the dinner table and waited for someone to ask what had happened, how I'd hurt myself. Often Deena wore bandages of her own, closer to her wrists, and these too were ignored.

We were a family that stayed on the surface, that didn't acknowledge our own cuts and scars, the sore and hurt places deep inside. We didn't talk about such things. We suffered in silence.

——

I don't know when it began. By the time we were in high school, Deena and I barely spoke. We hated each other once, for almost a year. Sitting in the same English class and never talking, never even looking at each other.

But when she began, I can't know, though it must have been in eleventh grade, when I was in tenth. That must have been when it began or when it became evident, when it began to take over. When it became bold. The first time I found puke in her room, in a plastic bag, all sweet and sticky and smelling like cake icing, I had no idea what I'd found. It wasn't talked about then, no one knew the words for it; no one even knew there were words for it: anorexia, bulimia.

Her room smelled sweet and rotten, like food going bad in the refrigerator. She smoked pot, that pungent smell leaking out from her room and into the hallway, and our mother thought the smell was incense, some strange Indian scent. She was so easy to deceive; she didn't want to know, so no one told her.

But Deena, sitting in her room, leaning over a plastic bag, her finger jammed down her throat, throwing it up, all that food and anger and ugly, suffocating love. Eyes watering, throat gagging, those sounds she covered with her stereo turned too high. How wonderful it must have been at first, to eat as much as she wanted and not have to worry about her weight, fitting into her jeans, those tight jeans we all wore. After years of constantly depriving herself, to finally be able to eat and not worry about calories and costs. It must have felt, in those first few months, as if she had found a miracle. It must have felt almost holy.

—⁓—

Maybe it was in imitation of Deena or maybe it was something I came up with myself, but by the middle of my sophomore year at high school I stopped eating. I starved my thin body even thinner, watched in fascination as my ribs jutted out, my collarbone stark against my neck. I spent hours in front of the mirror, dressed in only my underpants and sagging bra as I touched my chest and legs and arms. I loved the feel of my bones pushing up from my flesh, trying to free themselves. I became obsessed with eating less and less, with the empty, gnawing feeling in my stomach and the weakness that caused my head to spin, my eyes to blur. I loved the longing that struck at lunch when everyone else at the table ate. I inhaled the smells of oranges and peanut butter, of spaghetti and milk and thick, rich cheese. I inhaled it like a drug, like something forbidden.

It didn't take me long to realize that I didn't have the discipline for anorexia. I had always been greedy when it came to food, and even though I tried to starve myself, I was weak. I hated myself for this weakness, this lust, the way my mouth watered at the smell of food. I hated how my hands instinctively reached out, as if I was doomed to eat. At the same time, as with all loves, I was caught up in the thrill of this dichotomy, the way I both loved and hated food: loved it for its temptations and hated it for the betrayal my body made in accepting it.

Finally, I took pills to keep the hunger away. Tranquilizers and antidepressants the family doctor prescribed for what he referred to as my nervousness. I slept through the long afternoons and weekends, triumphant, when I finally woke up, that I made it through another day barely eating a thing.

───·◦·───

Before this, when we were younger and still close, Deena and I used to steal tomatoes from the garden, both of us sitting out in the dirt in our shorts, chests flat and tanned as a boy's. Feet bare, toes digging in the dirt, a stolen salt shaker in one of our pockets. The tomatoes so red they were almost purple, drooping over the vines with such abundance that we felt intoxicated; we couldn't stop eating. Not even when our tongues ached from the acid, when the roofs of our mouths were numbed dull and sore.

We were rich back then, young and silly enough to believe that we would always be nourished. We sat filthy with tomato stains, the smells of rotting cucumbers and peppers behind us, and we didn't talk or even touch. Still, we were close then, as close as we would ever be, sitting in the dirt, our mouths chewing, our faces held up to the sun.

One thing I was afraid of during those years was Deena's anger, how quickly she could turn and flatten me. She knew just what to say, the exact shape of my sensitive spots, those weak places over my skin I couldn't bear to touch. She probed these with a tone, a word, a motion of her eyes. We were linked so closely that we both knew the unmentionable things, the things that could destroy each other.

She never went that far, but she flirted and teased, leaning against the wall in my room, her tone sneering as she recited my flaws: My flat feet, my skinny legs, my lack of hips and breasts. My pointed face that looked like a rat's. My voice and the things that came out of my mouth. She could imitate me almost to the letter but in a higher, uglier tone, until my words sounded passive and questioning.

She followed me around the house, taunting me. No one intervened; maybe they didn't want her to turn on them. No matter what I did, homework or reading or even sitting in the living room watching television, she might be there whispering my faults like some type of omnipresent narrator.

It was absurd, really, but no one stepped in and told me otherwise, and before long, I started to wonder: Did I laugh funny, cough wrong? Were my feet ugly, was my hair hopeless, my voice too high and flat? I heard her voice in my head when she wasn't there, taunting me from a distance, and soon I started to view myself that way too, as if I were someone else, a character from a book, someone in third person.

Deena and I were caught, stuck, pulling and biting and gnawing to get away. We clawed and tugged, we laughed and wept and lashed out. We didn't have words for what we needed to say, so we said other things, we dug and slammed and cut ugly, jagged wounds in each other's psyches. It was unforgivable, the things we did and said to each other. But there was no other way. We both knew this. We understood this completely.

Winter nights, when the snow pressed against the house, the wind pushing drifts higher than the windowpanes, I ran around the cellar, the cement floor hard beneath my thin tennis shoes, the space heater throwing flames that did little to fight the chill. Running past the fireplace and the couch, across the softer surface of the braided rug and then the cement floor again as I loped around the pool table, the ping-pong table, and then over to the unfinished area and under the steps, past the gaping hole covered in plastic sheeting from the addition that had been built after my mother married my stepfather.

I ran two hundred, four hundred, six hundred laps, running until my feet ached and my legs shook, until my head throbbed and my eyes watered and my legs threatened to collapse, and still I didn't stop, couldn't stop, couldn't bear to walk back up the cellar steps, through the kitchen and rejoin the rest of the household.

It was overcast that day, sometime in October, the weather cool and breezy with a hint of warmth. I was sixteen and sitting in the school library, looking up information for a report. The next thing I knew, I was walking the six miles home in just my socks, my loafers left behind under the table, the heels pressed together as if waiting for my feet to return.

I walked over paved, country back roads until I reached our road, which was dirt, small pebbles pricking my feet. Once I reached the house, I crawled in my bedroom window. My mother was home, I could hear her out in the living room, the TV on. Occasionally she talked to herself. I felt embarrassed hearing her like that, when she thought no one was around. I quietly opened the bottle of pills the doctor gave me and swallowed them one by one, with small sips of Kool-Aid left beside my bed. By the time I finished, my tongue felt bruised and swollen. I lay down in the shadows behind my bed and closed my eyes. Colors swirled behind my eyelids and I realized that I was hungry. That was the last thing I thought of, food. I thought of potatoes and buttered corn and the thick, rich taste of meat in my mouth.

～❧～

Deena found me later that night, sneaking into my room to swipe one of my shirts and seeing my pale, naked feet sticking out from behind the bed. She screamed, that is what they told me later, that she screamed and grabbed me, hit me in the face and yelled my name. Shaking the empty bottle and pills and screaming, "How could you? How could you?"

I was rushed to the hospital, my stomach pumped. I hadn't taken enough to die, just to sleep for a long, long time, that is what the doctor said and that is what I wanted, to sleep for weeks, months. I longed for the heavy blackness, the sense of nothing that slips in between dreams.

I don't remember Deena or my mother or anything but the hospital lights scorching my eyes and the doctor telling me, in a bored and hurried voice, that my throat would be scratched from the tubes, that for a few days, it would hurt to swallow.

～❧～

Sometimes even now I'll remember the way that psych ward smelled, sharp and clean, like antiseptic, and behind that the sour, unwashed smell of longing. That's what we did all day: we kept ourselves as clean as they would allow as we longed for other things. To be home. To be able to eat crackers in bed and read whatever books we chose. We talked about food almost constantly, that's what it comes down to when you're locked up and monitored. You become like an animal, sneaky and sly, trying to feed yourself whatever way you can.

We were given pills, too many pills, in small paper cups each morning and evening, though the unlucky ones got them at noon also. We pushed these into our mouths, swallowed, and lifted our tongues to prove we had taken them. Then we traded the pills for the things we really wanted: chocolate, cigarettes, sex. We all smoked, even those of us who would never smoke again. There was nothing else to do, and those first few puffs were intoxicating; they made us almost giddy.

There was a group of us, five or sometimes six, all of us products of failed love and failed health. We watched soap operas and game shows, made crafts and strolled through the grounds single file, like a kindergarten class. But mostly we played cards and talked. We lied. We did this because we were scared, and because our truths were too intricate and interwoven to begin to dissect.

At night, I snuck off with a tall guy named Bill and lay in his narrow bed, snaking my cool, pale hands (for it was always cold in those rooms, we all wore sweaters and sometimes even coats, though the nurse and aides appeared immune to this coldness) down his chest. We were never caught, and soon we began taking bigger risks: meeting in the hallway, the bathroom, the meeting room with all the chairs in a circle as we pressed up against the wall and groped beneath each other's clothes. We didn't much like each other, but we needed one another. We needed the danger and the feigned thrill. We needed to believe we were diving headfirst inside desire, though in reality we were just scared, and desperate. We were both so young.

─ ⁍ ─

Was it there in that hospital that the dream started, the dream that has followed me through life, the one where I am trapped in a box, the sides too high for me to climb out? The box is slippery and cheap, and I tear through it with my hands, but outside is another box, and then another. I dream this dream over and over, and when I wake up, I can still see that goddamned box in my bedroom: gray and dirty and smelling of moldy dampness, like old garbage.

─ ⁍ ─

Deena came to visit every day I was in that hospital, standing or sitting beside me, smoking with that haughty look of someone scared out of her fucking mind but trying hard not to let it show. Sometimes she talked about school, the boy she was seeing. I'd show her the lopsided crafts I made in occupational therapy or describe the food they slapped on my tray during meals. Once we played pool, Deena's hands shaking as she rubbed chalk over her cue stick. I didn't ask why and she didn't tell me. Maybe she was taking speed or had been drinking before she came. Her breath often smelled ripe and fruity from the gum she chewed, and her lips were always chapped.

After I was released, we became kinder, almost tender toward one another. We rarely talked, we spent almost no time together, still it was there between us, each time we passed or accidentally brushed our arms in the hallway, a pulse like a heartbeat, a song only we could hear. We had always suspected that one of us would try to kill ourselves. It was an unspoken reality, and it had followed us around like a shadow. Now that it had been put to rest, we could go on and live our lives, though of course it wasn't that easy, and soon it was as if nothing had changed. I went to school, joined the track team, sent away for college applications. I had to see a psychologist once a week, my mother driving me into the city after school, both of us tense and angry and hating each other for the things we couldn't, must never, say to one another.

But I don't remember much about Deena during that time. I was fighting too hard to stay together, to pretend that I was okay. I thought that she was better but now I realize that she wasn't, that whatever had cleared between us couldn't make up for whatever else was going on inside of her head. She locked herself in her room, blared her music, smoked, and threw up while I sat alone in my room reading Sylvia Plath and writing poetry. I wore thick blue eye shadow and went out with a boy who was already in college, his pale, smooth body dancing above mine in the low light of his dorm room. With my skin pressed up against his, nothing else could touch me. Once, lying awake in bed, my mouth sore from his kisses, I heard Deena sneak in, so late it was almost morning, and I wondered if she had found a way to do the same, use boys, sex, her own treacherous body, if only for a few short hours or minutes, to get away.

※

Liver and onions. Wheaties with cold milk and strawberries. Pop-Tarts hot from the toaster, the icing burning my palms. I started eating again when I joined the track team in eleventh grade, and I ate regularly through my second year of college, when an injured knee forced me to stop running, and then I slowly stopped eating again, not completely but still, I withheld food, I kept myself away from food, from the briny taste of salt, the heavenly lift of sugar across my tongue. For years I did this, I punished myself this way.

※

When Deena was in college, I drove down to see her. I was getting ready to leave for college myself, in a few short months, escaping through two states, the farthest I had ever been. It was unimaginable, it was like a dream that I would finally do this: leave.

Deena lived in a dorm, in a room by herself. She'd had a roommate, but she had moved out. She needed to be by herself, she told me. My sister, strange then, not like she had been. Quiet, pale, nervous, glancing around as if afraid of being watched. Books all around the room, thick, sturdy, serious-looking books. Her mind clever and sly and quick. She would have made a good debater or public speaker, except that she was afraid to get up in front of a crowd, I could see that. Her fear. I could almost smell it on her.

I didn't know what she was afraid of. I didn't understand the way shame could reach down and strangle you, make you suddenly aware of every shortcoming, every flaw, magnifying everything until you become paralyzed, stuck with all your fears and ugliness. I didn't understand then, I was too young. It hadn't happened to me yet, though it would, in just a few short years. Maybe I knew this, maybe I recognized something in her posture or language, because I was tense all day, jumpy. I wanted to get away.

We didn't get to eat in the dining hall, the thing I had been looking forward to, a cafeteria with all those choices, all those possibilities. Instead, we walked to a small store and bought food, ate it alone in her room. I don't know if she threw it up afterward, though now I realize she probably did. We didn't talk to anyone the whole time, and I didn't think how unusual this was until later. The way the other girls said hello and quickly ducked away. How Deena carried her back so rigid, not looking at anyone.

That lonely room, all those books for company. It scared me. All day I felt so hungry, I couldn't stop thinking of food.

Michigan

After I left for college, I barely talked with Deena or anyone from my family. I was off in another state, running on the cross-country team and sleeping with men. I rarely allowed myself to think of where I came from. I pretended that it didn't matter, and before long I didn't even go back for vacations. I stayed in my college town, with this friend or that.

I fell in love with a man who was engaged to another woman and we met at night, riding our bikes through that dark town. We were careless and silly, riding no handed, chasing each other through the cemetery and around the tombstones. Our favorite path was down a big hill, almost half a mile long, no light, just that dark pavement flying past our handlebars. One small rock, a soda can, a piece of exhaust pipe and it would be all over, our bodies crashing down on that hard, unforgiving surface.

The speed and the danger were intoxicating. We couldn't get enough, riding faster and faster, daring each other to go farther: one-handed, eyes closed. One night my bike hit the curb while my eyes were closed, and as I wobbled and fought for balance, I suddenly thought of Deena, her white T-shirt leading me through the dark fields back home. I managed to steady myself and made it down, laughing shakily in the safety of the streetlights. But something had changed inside of me, and in bed that night with that man, I struggled as if fighting something vast and unmentionable.

Two weeks later, I took off with another man. As if to show my lover, as if to say to him, "How dare you, how dare you love me!"

When I was nineteen, I called Deena. She was in graduate school at the time, her decline already begun, but I didn't notice it,

I didn't suspect a thing. I was too young and selfish. What I needed was money for an abortion. Two hundred dollars. Of course my sister didn't have it. She was poorer than I was, waitressing and going to school at night. I stood at that phone booth and shivered, the receiver pressed hard to my ear.

She told me to call home, to make something up, a lie about rent or crashing the car. Blood money, she said. You deserve it.

I knew I could never do that, but still I didn't hang up. I listened to her suck a cigarette as I stalled, afraid to let go of the phone.

"Honey," she said, the only one who called me that. "Honey, are you sure . . . ."

But I hung up. I couldn't bear to hear what she might say next.

~⋄~

My senior year of college, I lived in a basement room of a large, old house with four other women. I didn't know them well, though they were kind, and oftentimes we all sat in the living room, on the sagging furniture that smelled of other people's dogs, and watched television while bitching about our classes. Before midterms, we ate huge bags of M&M's and Snickers and worried about getting fat.

Because most of my classes were late in the afternoon, I snooped through their things after they left in the morning. I was ashamed of doing this, and every time, I promised myself it would be the last. But I couldn't stop. I crept into their rooms with my heart pounding, my mouth almost watering from the thrill of discovery. I read their letters, slipped their clothes on over my nightgown, pulled on their socks, their shoes. I liked to dress in their clothes and then stand in front of the mirror, pretending I was them. I tried to imagine what it would feel like to be normal, to go to bed at night and then wake up in the morning without feeling the need to fight through the day.

What I liked best was eating their food. I'd sneak upstairs late at night and steal it out of the refrigerator. Then I'd take it down to my room, turn on the lamp, sit in front of the mirror, and watch myself as I stuffed their food into my mouth. This excited me, and oftentimes when I finished, I touched myself, my hands smeared with chocolate or covered with salt from corn chips. I lay there in front of the mirror, the taste of their food still in my mouth, and when I was finished, I licked my fingers clean, curled up on the rug and worried about what I would say when they got up in the morning and discovered their cake or sandwich or bag of snacks gone. I always bought them more and could have easily bought for myself as well, but I never did. It tasted better when it belonged to someone else.

In the dream, I'm sleeping in my childhood bedroom. A noise, and I sit up, wrap the blankets tight around my fist. Footsteps out in the hall, moving slowly, stealthily. Coming closer and then stopping. My heart pounding, that awful silence, no sound, just that god-paralyzed pause.

Just when I think I'm safe, the doorknob twists, and I jam the wad of blankets into my mouth, trying to remember if I've locked the door. If he can get in.

That's when I wake up. Sweating. Crying. All this time, years and years later, and I'm still afraid of such a simple, normal thing: a door opening.

Back then, I knew nothing about sex, real sex, the kind that's tender and long and slow. What we did, what I did with those boys who were still years away from becoming men, what we did was fuck. This way and that. Our breaths tasting of beer, our clothes reeking of pot and last night's sweat. In our single, college beds, or one of our roommates' beds. Sheets dirty, our passion feigned and desperate and not lasting nearly as long as it should have.

I enjoyed it in a physical way. It was like running, something athletic; a workout. My body moving this way and that, muscles tensing. He came, and sometimes if I was lucky, I came also. Then it was over. We didn't stay in bed, we didn't lie in each other's arms and talk, we got up and what we did, what I did with those men, was eat. We'd eat in those filthy, small college apartment kitchens, old takeout food or things made quickly from boxes. Sitting at the table, clearing a spot through the dirty dishes, and sometimes we ate off of paper towels when there were no dishes clean. We sat there and ate french fries or cold pizza, pancakes still soggy in the middle, and drank milk that tasted slightly sour and stayed heavy on my tongue for hours afterward. That's what I would remember, when I finally got back to my own bed, sneaking in quietly so as not to wake my roommate. I lay down there in the dark, and what I thought of wasn't the man, or the sex, or the noises either of us had made. What I thought of was that milk, so white and pure when I poured it in the paper cup, and the betrayal, the affront of finding out that it was sour, that it had gone bad.

～♋～

Deena and I liked to write. Both of us outcasts, Deena because of her eating and her madness, and me because of my voice, which often broke and stuttered. We were different, never quite fitting in, though I could pretend to, turning this way and that until the shame wore me down. This shame never lets up, never entirely, following me around like a weary shadow, growing and expanding until every part of me is washed in it: My hair, teeth, skin. My voice, mouth, breasts, thighs, cunt.

But when I write, I am free, off somewhere else, seeing and hearing and smelling through someone else's senses. A voyeur, like the way I look in the windows of the houses I pass when I walk the dog at night, curious and jealous of other people's lives. All those people sitting around the dining room table, mouths moving, plates of food passing as I stand outside in my heavy winter coat, the dog tugging on the leash. Surely, they know something I don't, possess a secret where I have only silence.

～⌒～

After I graduated from college, I headed out West with a boyfriend. I had a scholarship offer to a graduate school back East but I gave it up, I shrugged it off for a chance to live in wide open spaces, skies so blue it was like a dream.

We left Michigan in the autumn and headed toward Flagstaff, where we'd decided to live. We chose our location randomly, recklessly, because it was in the mountains and because it was small, with a good outdoor community. We pored over maps for hours, imagining the life we would soon lead.

We drove for three days, my boyfriend's old Labrador retriever drooling over my legs. We hit Colorado in the dark and camped out in a field, waking early in the morning to the sound of horses galloping past. I crawled out of the tent to the surprise of mountains rising like a cry, like something fierce and gnawing at my belly. I knew without a doubt that I was staring into the face of God.

"I'll never settle for less," I told myself as I rolled up my sleeping bags, walked past the horses and back down to the road.

And though my life was shit for years, though I left that man and countless others, I never once left the mountains.

The West

For years I was angry, so angry I could barely stand it. I took this out on everyone. I blamed my past, my job, my family, my boyfriend, even God. Once, walking through the streets in northern New Mexico with a man I had just betrayed, we stopped in a church. It was silent and cool. My veins throbbed against my wrist until I thought I would go mad from it all, my blood, that ugly red energy. I leaned over, opened his pants and took him in my mouth. In the background, I heard the hiss of a lawn sprinkler and the howl of a dog. Afterward, I wanted to run through the aisles and break statues. I wanted to pee on the pew, destroy something, anything.

On the way out, I spit in the holy water. It pleased me to think of someone dabbing it over their forehead thinking it was sacred and, instead, all my failures sticking to their skin. When we got back to the house we were renting for the summer, I fucked that man on the living room floor, meanly, almost savagely, counting each stroke as if in penance.

I would probably be dead if it weren't for my friend Denny. Or maybe not, maybe I'm stronger than I think. Still, all those years I wandered from place to place, and he always offered me his home. "Stay," he would say, and I would. For a while. Stay there with his golden hair and his tanned shoulders. But I would leave again.

He was beautiful and strong back then. The kind of man you might see in a Western, hoisting a saddle over a horse before tipping his hat to a lady. The guy in white, who not only saves the day but remembers to brush down the horse afterward. So good he's almost bland, almost boring.

I met him in college, left him over and over and finally for good when I was almost thirty. In between, there were more than the usual lies and acts of betrayal, fights where we threw books and once, in a horrible late-night rage, a bullet whizzing past my ear so close I could hear the sound it made through the air.

We lived in Michigan, New Mexico, and Arizona, finally ending up in Alaska, his dream, not mine. But I followed him. We followed each other across the West like desperate pilgrims. Hitchhiking across the country, heavy packs on our backs, our armpits reeking no matter how much deodorant we slathered beneath them each morning. I wore shorts. Tank tops. My tanned shoulders and long legs. When we had problems getting rides, in those long stretches between towns, Denny would hide in the weeds and I'd hike up my shirt so my stomach showed, my thumb held out. It wouldn't take long before someone would stop, some man, and then we'd both climb in, get a ride to the next town or the next.

One man offered us a room in Durango, another one in Vegas, but we spread our sleeping bags out over the ground instead, under the stars, so that before we fell asleep, we could watch the sky spread out before us like something magnificent and pure, something we had never seen before.

Each night we did this, until the mosquitos began appearing. Even then I'd often sleep on that hard ground outside of the tent, risking the wrath of bites for a glimpse of the night sky, out in a field or valley, mountainside or next to a lake. One night we watched a shooting star arch through the sky and we held our breaths, we stayed awake half the night as if to prolong the moment, make it last. But it was gone, and that was the last time we saw a shooting star together.

All those years after I graduated from college and roamed around out West, Deena and I kept in touch via the phone. These conversations weren't easy. Deena could be difficult, was often difficult, I won't lie, won't do that to her, gloss her over, make her into someone she wasn't. How she would have hated that, how she would have sneered, lifted her hand and waved her cigarette in my face.

"Just say what you want," she'd mock, followed by a shrug, a little forced laugh. Because we can't help it, we'll never be able to help it: we come from a family afraid to tell the truth.

By the time we finished college she was talking about things that hadn't happened, couldn't have happened, crazy things: people killed and buried in the space beneath her apartment building; a boyfriend killing women and hiding them in her car trunk; how she sometimes woke up covered with blood and knew someone was coming in at night and hurting her.

What do you do, what do you say when someone tells you such things? You bury your nails so deep in your thighs that you bleed. You listen and afterward, you hang up the phone slowly, the receiver banging the desk. You pray. You cry. You hate yourself for it but still you do it. You slowly, ever so slowly, you turn away.

INTERLUDE 2

Anchorage, Alaska

Flying home to Deena's funeral with my son, who is nine at the time, I read *Wasted: A Memoir of Anorexia and Bulimia* by Marya Hornbacher. The flight is choppy over Canada, and while my son sleeps, his head warm on my shoulder, I think about death, worry that the plane might crash, imagine that long and cold drop from the sky. Then I think that no, Deena won't let that happen, she'll hold us up. The rest of the flight I feel calmer, as if my son and I are floating in my sister's palm.

Years later, when I'm a feature writer at a newspaper in Anchorage, I contact Hornbacher for a book review I'm doing of her second book, fiction this time but equally beautiful, the type of book you read in small pieces. I tell her how *Wasted* saved my life after my sister died, how I held it in my hands like a Bible, slept with it beneath my pillow. How it comforted me that Hornbacher was able to pull herself up and live, even though my sister died.

I don't remember what Hornbacher said, most likely the usual things an author says when confronted with a reader who feels as if she's been deeply touched. Writers write more for themselves than others, I know this now. Still, it was nice connecting with her, if only briefly. It made my Deena's death that much more intimate, as if I had been on a journey with her, as if I were offered glimpses of her life through someone else's words.

~ ༄ ~

Back when my son was young I picked herbs and hung them to dry in the laundry room. I brewed tea for when we were sick or sad or feeling anxious: chamomile, red clover, yarrow. I made chickweed tonic, violet cough syrup. I dug dandelion roots, picked rose petals to scent oils and lotions, and cooked up jams from currants, blueberries, raspberries. Once we snuck into a neighbor's yard at night to pick the raspberries they never used, thick and nearly dropping off the bush, so sweet and succulent that we became intoxicated, ran all the way home, raspberries falling to the ground like rain. Rolling in the grass in our yard, laughing, holding our bellies, juice smeared over our faces, our fingers stained. His face, in the late summer twilight, glowing like the moon.

—◦c—

The body remembers every hurt, every cut and bruise, every slap and sting, every betrayal, every disappointment, every loss. The morning I hear Sarah McLachlan's "Angel" on the radio as I'm driving out to run the Middle Fork Trail with the dog, I begin to cry, I don't know why. Then I remember: it's Deena's birthday. The tears come harder, and it's like magic, crying that way; it's an odd type of wisdom.

What I want, more than anything else at that moment, is to hear her voice. I want to see her, touch her, hold her hand, place my palm against her cheek, feel the warmth of her skin against mine. I want all of this, yes, but what I desire the most is the sound of her voice, that husky, sardonic tone, dipping down and then rising slightly up at the end: *Hey, Cin, remember the time we . . .*

I sit in the car and wait, but there is nothing. No voice, no hint of a ghost, not even a memory. Only Sarah McLachlan's voice, sweet and pure and filling my ears like water.

—◦c—

Late summer, my son and I pick blueberries out at Flattop Peak. We take the dog and hike up around Blueberry Hill and weave through thin trails that intersect across the side of the mountain. It is early evening, the air still light but beginning to dim. We have plastic containers with us, and Ziploc plastic bags, and we kneel on the cold ground and pick the small blueberries that fleck the hill with milky blue-purple dots. My son eats more than he picks, he sits on the ground, berries staining his pants, and eats blueberries and crowberries, his mouth stained, his fingernails lined with dirt.

I wear shorts, and something bites my legs, though I don't feel it at the time. When I'm alone with my son and the dog and the mountains, with the twilight slowly fading and the air becoming colder, I feel nothing but a thick and fat contentment that mixes with the tart tastes of berries so that whenever I think of happiness, it carries the surprise of wild blueberries against my tongue.

DENYING

—⁀⚬⚓⚬⁀—

Words from the Dead

So no, I wasn't actually shocked or stunned to get your call.

—from Deena's notebooks

Tucson, Arizona

I like to think it was a miracle that my older sisters and I ended up in the desert for one year together, in that dry heat and sky that went on forever. We were still young, in our mid-to-late twenties, all of us in separate apartments but still together, as together as we knew how to be. Smells of sage and chaparral, and when it rained, the earth sucked up the water with a greed that shamed me, as if it knew how I felt as I lay with all the men I met. As if it knew how hungry and thirsty I was, not for sex or even love but for touch. For someone touching me.

Dawn, my oldest sister, worked as a nurse and lived with a boyfriend who treated her badly, and Deena lived in an old apartment by the university, water bugs the size of my fist crawling out from beneath the toilet. In the evenings I'd go over and sit with her out on the steps. We walked a lot. She didn't have a car, though I did, an old Mercury Comet I'd driven down from where I had been living in Alaska. I'd tell her about my trip, the way the sky looked in the Yukon, and the taste of water from rivers so cold my tongue ached.

Deena wore her hair short and curly as a boy's. She was thin when she first got to Tucson but slowly put on weight. Not a lot, but enough to keep her going. We read books together or walked down Fourth Avenue and past the thrift stores. Shopping for bargains, for something to transform us into the lives we really wanted.

Even now, when I think of Deena, I think of the smell of old clothes and the deep, parched silence of the desert at night. And the men I saw afterward, how I slipped into their houses, their cars. Leaving Deena behind and running to the desperate struggle of bodies and semen and sometimes blood. One lover used to iron his sheets and I'd slip into his bed, those sheets so cool and smooth it was like water, like diving into a pool.

The desert! Waves of heat in the afternoon blasting across my skin like an oven door suddenly opened. Blisters over my heels, hands chapped, legs tanned the color of wood. In the afternoons I didn't work, I hiked up in the mountains, found a warm, flat rock, stripped off my clothes and lay down, just me and all that sky. Sometimes I read or slept. Other times I stared at the sky for hours, no clouds, just blue stretching out forever.

Deena in a plaid shorts set, colors bright and almost garish against her legs, so pale and thin that it was frightening. It was painful to watch her walk, her neck long and corded with veins, her arms wasted away to almost nothing.

We walked, sitting down often. She said she was thirsty, that her legs hurt, that it was just too damned hot. But really, she couldn't walk for long, she was too weak, she'd gone too long without food. We walked, stopped, walked, stopped, a rhythm I'd rediscover years later when my son took his first steps.

All around us, in that desert, everything was muted shades of browns and tans and pinks, and Deena was so bright, like some type of malnourished bird. I wanted to slap her, my hand hitting the hard expanse of her bones, those bones waiting to pop up through her skin. Shake her hard, kicking her, throwing her across the street. I was furious with her, I didn't want anything to do with her, with this weak, needy person my sister had become. Yet I continued walking beside her, nodding at whatever she said. I wanted to leave, get away. I wanted to grab her hand, squeeze it tight. I wanted to hold on forever. I wanted us both to disappear.

He had a waterbed, a picture of John Wayne on the wall by the dresser. Before we fucked he'd throw his bathrobe over the frame. "Don't want the Duke watching," he'd say, and sometimes he wore a cowboy hat, strutted around naked like a cowboy.

"Ain't I the dude?" he said, sticking his stomach out, snarling his lip up, trying to look hard and mean.

He was nice, that one. He had a picture of his daughter in the living room, wearing one of those frilly dresses, her chubby hands folded as if in prayer. Praying he'd come back. His wife in another state, they were separated. I didn't understand then, I was so young, running from one man to another. I didn't have a child yet, I didn't understand how that kind of love can strangle you, a noose around the neck if you're away too long.

We played games. Acted things out.

In the mornings, I lay in bed and watched him iron his work clothes, blue oxford shirts, perfect creases down the arms. He was nice, that man. So sweet and good.

I left him, ran off with someone else. Not a word or an explanation. I simply left.

Memory is so elusive, so strange and dreamy and compelling: how can you ever know if you've gotten it right, remembered what really happened instead of what you wanted or hoped to have happened?

Maybe none of this is true, maybe some of it is true; maybe it's all a dream, a fantasy, the words I use to explain myself late at night when I can't sleep.

Already I am forgetting things. "Remember when you said this, did that, went there?" my son asks, and I shake my head, because really, I have no recollection, none at all, though if I think hard enough, I can remember a vague outline, a dim, hazy shadow.

"Remember this?" my son demands. "And that?" Sometimes of course I do remember, and sometimes what I remember is so different from his version that he shakes his head sadly.

"You don't remember right," he says, somewhat accusingly. He sees this as a betrayal, a way of separating myself from him, and because of that, he needs to see it as my fault. "You can't remember, can you?" he challenges, and I nod, agree, because of course it is true, it's something that he'll understand when he's older: that vast selectiveness of our own memories, how we hoard our hurts and disappointments to our chests while forgetting what doesn't adhere to our own stuttering self-concepts. We do this unconsciously, totally unaware of how we are layering or fabricating. And if you asked us, we would swear, swear on the Bible, on our lives, on the lives of our children, that everything, every single word is true, that yes, it really happened like that, and just like that.

~ ∂σ ~

Deena carried a knapsack with her everywhere she went, filled with food: Diet Pepsi, saltine crackers, butterscotch candies. For weeks these were the only things she ate, along with spoonfuls of dried protein powder she bought in canisters at the health food store.

She ate slowly, sparingly, allowing herself small nibbles instead of bites, her spoon turned over and pressed against her tongue, as if to allow herself every slight crumb. It was maddening, watching her eat, witnessing such a thing: the laborious care she took in separating everything into neat piles and how she ate one small bite at a time and always in the same order—protein powder, sip of Diet Pepsi, half of a saltine cracker. It could take her more than an hour to eat a few bites, each one followed by the slow, greedy suck of the spoon against her tongue.

She never sat at a table but on the living room floor, cross-legged, as if in some bizarre form of meditation. I couldn't stand watching her eat and often slipped outside and sat on the porch, my hands clapped over my ears to escape the sound of her spoon tapping the bowl and then the long interval of pause.

"Take another bite," I screamed inside of my head. "Pick up your fucking spoon and take another bite!"

But I remained quiet, sitting in the clear desert night. Throwing stones across the yard, picking my toenails, trying to read novels by the dim porch light. I imagined stomping back inside, grabbing Deena by the throat, shaking her mouth open, and then pouring in the rest of the food. I was so angry, so furious—what right did she have to eat so slowly, to act as if food meant nothing, as if she needed nothing, could sustain on air alone?

"Liar." I wanted to slap her, kick her, sob against her bony, pale shoulders. "Goddamned fucking liar."

I sat outside until she was finished. Often, she threw it back up, I could hear her in the bathroom, the fan going, the water running, and when she came out, that stale smell around her lips she couldn't brush away with toothpaste.

***

It's no wonder the man I loved then was cold, unattached, able to think only of himself. "I love you," he whispered into my hair, my stomach, that slippery place between my legs. But he didn't. Neither one of us did, though we said it, screamed it out, swore over and over.

He had been married, thought he knew more than I did, he acted fatherly and resentful, he loved my skin, my body, my youth, but he also hated it, resented it; he was so much older, so much more ordinary. In the summer, with my skin tanned and my body revealed beneath the skimpy clothes I favored, people looked at me, men and women. Blond hair down to my ass, waist so small he could lock his hands around it and still have room left over. I offered my body up to him, over and over; it was the only thing I had of value, the only thing I knew how to give. I offered him my breasts, my belly, my cunt. I wrapped my legs around his head, his hips, his shoulders, held him tight.

It wasn't pleasure, it wasn't even close, it was something else. Deeper, darker. We rarely laughed together, didn't even talk much. We had very little to say beyond the language of our bodies.

In some strange way, he reminded me of Deena.

———⁂———

The monsoons came in July, the sky clouding over each after-noon, and then the rains, abruptly, almost without warning, water falling from the sky like a gift. And the way it smelled, fresh and clean, almost sweet. I'd ride my bike out of town, run through the sand, my shoes kicked off, that wet earth sucking my toes. It was exhilarating, to be so wet, my skin cold, my face lifted to the sky.

I liked to drive up in the mountains, hike up by the washes, sit and wait through the rains until the roar of the water. It was so sudden that I shivered, torrents of water rushing forward. It was mesmerizing to lean down as close as I dared, the water muddy and filled with stones and dirt, uprooted scrub brush, and once a rabbit, its body tumbling over and over. And always the urge to jump in, fling myself into that water, my body hitting rocks, bruising and soaring. It would be something to die that way, baptized by that water.

Minutes after the rain stopped, the water began to disap-pear. This happened so quickly it was hard to believe, a short hour later, that it had ever rained to begin with. The washes dried up until I could walk through them, debris scratching my legs. The air heavy with a lingering moistness, the sky still overcast. I stayed out as long as I dared, it was such a welcome relief from the heat.

Those years I slept curled up in a tight ball on my side, fetal position, arms crossed against my breasts, ankle tight between my legs: fortification, like a chastity belt. Like screaming: Stay away. Don't touch me.

Sleep is so defenseless, isn't it? We are unarmed, vulnerable. Anything can happen as we sleep, our bodies spread out and open. Yet it is a risk we willingly take each night. We lie down, pull the covers up. Maybe the sheets smell of fabric softener or grass from drying outside on the clothesline. We close our eyes, drift off, trusting, against all logic, against all odds, that we will be safe. That nothing will happen. That no one will touch us or steal things from us. That we will eventually wake up, the same as when we fell asleep, hours before.

It took me years to learn how to surrender to sleep, to give myself up to the unknown, to that seductive yet unpredictable void. Even now I surround my sleeping area with crystals, beach stones, driftwood, talismans against my own vulnerabilities, my own helplessness.

There were times when I was so depressed I couldn't do the small, simple things people take for granted. Plant flowers. Cook a meal. Iron a blouse. I could run and work out, ride my bike, swim eighty laps across the pool. I could work double shifts and stay out all night with a man and work all the next day without a break, but I couldn't do a week's grocery shopping, send a card, answer the phone. I was too afraid. I felt too damned heavy.

I remember not being able to wind the cord around the vacuum cleaner after I finished cleaning. Such a small thing, really, but I couldn't do it, couldn't make myself lean down and wind that cord around the plastic knobs on the back of the machine. I left it like that, cord tangled as I stuffed it back in the closet. Once a lover vacuumed the rug after he spilled cereal and I watched in amazement as his arms wound that cord quickly and carelessly around the vacuum cleaner.

"You don't have to do that," I said, and he shrugged, kept on going.

The incident left me seething with resentment. It took me years after I left him to understand that I was jealous, not only of him but everyone. I was afraid of the things I couldn't do, afraid that it meant that something was wrong with me.

There was, of course. I just wasn't ready to admit it yet.

———

The first time I ate an avocado, I was in a restaurant in California with my cold-hearted lover, and I wore a white dress that swirled off my tanned shoulders, my sun-bleached hair shining down my back. Five slices of avocado nestling by my sandwich, the outer layer dark, the inner fruit a pale green with hints of yellow. I picked up a piece, that slippery, moist fruit, and held it to my mouth, the smell pleasant yet unpleasant, the taste smooth and buttery with a pungent aftertaste. And I thought, with wonder and fear, as I ate the first slice and then the next: This is how it would taste to go down on a woman. This is how I taste. This is me.

———

In the afternoons I rode my bike over to Deena's apartment, lying around her pool during the worst of the heat. Sitting in her small apartment the nights I didn't work, talking about everything but never that. We never mentioned her weight. Or food. It was as if they didn't exist.

Our mother sent money each month and Dawn also pitched in but even so, Deena was poor, applying for food stamps and collecting coupons. Her money never lasted the month, and when it was low, we prowled the supermarkets, tearing off labels and wrappers so that Deena could mail in rebate coupons: a dollar here, a couple of dollars there. We laughed doing this, sometimes laughed so hard we had to run out of the store. But later, in her shabby apartment, both of us sitting cross-legged on the couch, I'd watch her addressing envelopes, a greedy and hopeful look on her face, and I'd have to escape to the bathroom to keep from crying.

Because something was wrong with Deena, something beyond her refusal to eat. There was something broken and fearful about her, something manic yet suffocating. She talked too much one day, and the next barely said a word. She was like a bird that had flown into a window, stunned and scared. She couldn't sleep nights, even when I stayed over. Old fears, bad dreams. I'd curl up in a heap of old blankets down on the floor, and after the house quieted down, she'd begin to talk, her voice low, the refrigerator humming around her words. I can't remember what she said, only that it was comforting to hear her voice, to fall asleep knowing she was awake up on the couch, smoking cigarettes and staring out the window.

Once I woke and found her standing by the window, staring out. All the lights on, the reflection of her face staring back at me from the glass. Shoulders rigid, mouth parted, eyes wide. I don't know what she saw, what she was looking for. I said her name softly and she jumped, the muscles in her neck thick and knotted.

I sat up with her until I couldn't stay awake any longer and then I dragged my blankets closer and curled up beside the couch, smells of her cigarettes and old dust. In the morning she begged me to stay while she slept, said she couldn't stand being alone, so I stayed for a few more hours, sitting in the living room and reading.

I slipped out late in the morning, running down the walk-way and getting on my bike, pedaling furiously back to my own apartment, filled with both exhilaration and relief, as if I had gotten away with something, as if I had escaped.

———

For years I was afraid of houses. Moving from one place to another. Even in college, I couldn't stay put, moving every semester, often in the middle of the semester. That trapped feeling, like suffocating, like not being able to breathe.

I never spoke about this to Deena but I think she would have understood. She didn't move as often, but she did move around. We both did. Like orphans, trying to find a place to stay, a place where we fit.

I remember them all: those apartments and houses, those rented rooms in someone's attic, those basement apartments. Cold or too hot. Damp or so dry my nose bled. My bed pushed up against this wall or that; it was important to be able to press my back against the wall, to have something solid between myself and my body. If I could have, I would have barricaded myself in my bed, walls all around, a locked door, lights blaring at the sound of a voice trying to push in.

Most of those years, in college and traveling through the West, I had insomnia. Eyes opened through the long and horrible night. The night passing so slowly, so ploddingly, my eyes aching, my heart thumping in my chest. An agonizing, ugly, deadly slowness. I took pills, saw doctors. They didn't believe I could stay awake for so long, two, sometimes three nights without sleep. The pills helped for a few weeks and then I would have to take more, and more. My head on fire, my eyes opened and staring at the door. Three o'clock, four, five—still unable to sleep.

But only indoors. Outside, camping or dragging blankets out into the yard, I closed my eyes and fell right to sleep. I felt safe out there, with the wind and trees and sky. All those stars burning through my dreams.

I worked the evening shift at the Village Inn on Speedway Boulevard and spent afternoons with Deena or hiking in the desert. I passed lizards and rattlesnakes and once a tarantula, scurrying across the path in front of my foot.

One night I came home from work to find two police sitting in my small kitchen. I was living in a junior apartment, the bedroom separated from the living room by a wall partition that didn't reach the ceiling. My oldest sister was with them and rushed over, grabbed my arm. The police seemed uncomfortable. They explained that the man in the apartment behind mine had been spying on me, that he'd drilled holes in the bathroom and bedroom walls, that he invited friends over to watch me shower and use the toilet. One of these friends contacted the apartment manager, who called my sister and the police.

The police showed me the holes, small areas by the bed and near the bathroom mirror. I sat down on the couch, stunned. The police asked questions, recommended that I sleep somewhere else until the man had been picked up. Dawn was furious and demanded that they press charges. That night I slept on her sofa, which smelled of dog and old food. I moved back to my apartment the next day, the holes freshly mended, white splotches that stuck out on the walls like ugly shouts. The man was released later that week. I came across him as he was moving out of his apartment. He leered at me, raised his eyebrows, asked how I was in a mocking voice.

I was still so young. I knew how to fight for physical boundaries but not emotional and especially not sexual ones. No one had taught me to say no, to value my body, to believe that it was mine, that it belonged to me. I should have slapped that man, spit in his face, kicked him in the balls. I should have released my anger, told him what he could do with the fucking holes he drilled in the fucking walls.

Instead, I nodded and smiled. Dawn wanted the landlady to let me out of my lease, but I didn't want to move. I couldn't comprehend what this man had done, that he had violated my sense of privacy and my body.

I couldn't understand this. I truly thought that it was no big deal.

⁓ ᧔ ⁓

Deena called me at work and asked me to stop by on my way home, said that she needed to show me something. She lived in a smaller apartment about a mile from mine, her bed tucked against the far wall. There was music playing when I walked in, every light on.

"Look." She grabbed Chuckie, the large calico stray she took in. She placed a pencil against the table rim and the cat batted it down. She played this game over and over, laughing each time.

A few days later she couldn't find Chuckie and called in a panic. I biked over, and we searched outside, shaking the food box. Later, we heard a thud in the kitchen, followed by a muffled cry, and Deena discovered that she accidentally closed him in the cupboard while he slept. She picked him up, hugged him against her shoulder.

I like to remember her like that, holding her cat, his large paws kneading her thin, thin back. Her heart was soft like that. She took in strays and later adopted three homeless dogs. I knew she would never have children and it comforted me that she had found something to love, something smaller and warmer, something that needed her, that would always love her back.

⁓ ᧔ ⁓

Deena asked me one night, as we sat in the dark by her apartment's swimming pool, her voice pondering, almost whimsical.

She wondered why she had been so mean to me back when we were in high school.

"I wonder why I hated you so much," she said.

The underwater swimming pool lights shimmered blue. I stared at them and then shrugged. I expected she would apologize, but she didn't. We sat side by side, not talking. Really, I suppose, there was nothing more to say.

The moon was almost full that night I spent down in Oak Creek Canyon with a lover. The air cool, no sounds but the wind and behind it, the steady movement of the creek. I followed his shadow over the stones, so cool now that the sun had gone down. It was as if we were lost, back in time. There was nothing to orient us, to tell us where we were, only that we were surrounded by rock, in a center so deep it was as if we had disappeared.

The wall of the canyon glowed white in the moonlight, smooth and clear. Our presence meant nothing to it. We were specks, blinks. I leaned my head back, opened my mouth, and licked those old rocks, those gritty flecks of dirt.

Deena was married, the only one of us brave enough to do that, to take that leap. Strange when you think about it, four daughters and only one married. It lasted, how many years? Seven? Eight? It's so easy to lose track.

He was a shy, fumbling man who talked too much. Tall, dark haired, boyish. I can't remember how Deena met him, but suddenly he was there, in her life. They seemed happy then, in the beginning when we all lived in Tucson. They moved in together, in the lower apartment in my building. I would go over in the evenings, sit reading while my sister drank Diet Pepsi and smoked. Both of us reading. He was at work, though sometimes he was there on the couch with us, talking, but neither one of us paid much attention to him. He used to sew bears for her, though, little teddy bears the size of her hand, the stitching clumsy, the material bunched and scattered at the seams. But still, it was tender and sweet. It embarrassed Deena, yet she kept those bears for years, still had some when she died.

After I left Arizona and moved back up to Alaska, Deena's husband joined the navy and they moved around the country: Maryland, Florida, Washington. She called sometimes, always at night. I was living with Denny then, had been living with him on and off for almost half of my life. When Deena called, I stretched out on the shabby, dog-smelling couch, our old Labrador retriever curled up at my feet, and I closed my eyes as we talked. We didn't say much. Even then I knew she was lonely, needed someone to listen to her, needed to throw her voice out just to hear that she was still alive. I knew, because I often felt the same way myself.

In Maryland, Deena seemed, if not happy, more content than she had ever before. She worked two waitressing jobs, took the dogs for long walks, read stacks of books from the library. A few years after they moved there, she broke her leg while walking the dogs. A car hit her, and she was on crutches for months, her leg in a long, white cast. She sent pictures, which I taped on the refrigerator and immediately forgot about.

Now I wonder: Maybe her leg just snapped, maybe she made up the story. Maybe she was walking and it just twisted wrong and broke. She was still throwing up, and she refused to eat anything other than white foods: oatmeal, protein powder, crackers. Maybe she fell, heard the crack and, unable to believe her bones could break so easily, that she had the bone density of a sixty-year-old woman, made up the story about the car. She told so many stories that it's impossible to untangle what was true and what was false. Like so many things, they were all true, in a sense, and all lies.

I was lonely those years, lonely and scared and hungry. I wanted so many things, but I wouldn't let myself have them. I was sure that anything I touched would fall apart and rot. There was something inside of me, something rusty and ugly and smelly, and if I let anyone get too close, they would feel, taste, smell, see it. I fucked men and left them, had casual friends at work, but my sisters were the only people I socialized with. I felt safe with them. I didn't have to pretend I was okay, didn't have to act happy and carefree. I could be sullen and depressed and moody. I could be myself.

When I fell in love with a man I knew I couldn't keep, I became pregnant instead. This happened while camping in the mountains of Northern California. Lying in a sleeping bag, the moon casting shadows across the ground until it was like being underwater, everything outlined in silver. I crawled into his sleeping bag, the heat of his skin and the way his mouth tasted of stale cigarettes and wine. I devoured him, my hair across his face, I was wild from the wind, from the things I wanted.

Once he slumped back to sleep, I walked outside. The sky was beginning to lighten and there was a moment when the sun rose yet the moon held firm, when it was both morning and night. I crouched down, slipped my diaphragm out of my body and buried it in the dirt.

After that, all I had to do was wait.

I wanted to keep her, but I wouldn't allow myself to. I was sick with wanting, so sick I couldn't keep anything down, not even water. I lay in bed all day counting the hours until night, when the nausea eased and I wandered alone down by the wash, the air smelling of heated rocks.

I don't know how I knew it was a girl, but I did, and soon I was dreaming of her in the different stages of her life: a toddler pulling boxes and plates off a kitchen counter; a schoolgirl, socks sagging down around her thin ankles; a young woman, face beautiful, secretive and uncertain. I found myself waiting for these dreams, longing for them with that intense, almost shameful way we always long for the things we know we cannot keep.

When I told the man I loved, the man I thought I loved, that I was pregnant, there was a long pause. He was a truck driver and out on the road at the time and so I told him over the phone.

"It's not mine," he said.

Then he hung up. He called back later that night and the next and the next, trying to convince me to have an abortion. "You're not ready to have a child," he said. "You need to grow up first."

A few days later he changed his tactic, said that if I had the baby, it would be deformed or retarded. I wasn't eating enough, he said. "How would you take care of a deformed child?" he asked. "You can't even take care of yourself."

I cried and cried after these phone calls, and before long he wore me down; the morning sickness wore me down; the heat wore me down. I asked him for money to pay for half of the abortion.

"It's not mine," he said, slamming down the phone.

I ended up dancing at a topless club to make the money. I shook my sore, bloated breasts in men's faces.

"This is what I deserve," I thought as a fat businessman slipped a five-dollar bill in my G-string. "This is who I really am."

I went by myself. I didn't want to see anyone's face, didn't want to have to meet anyone's eyes. I lay down on that cold, awful table, my feet in the stirrups, the bleached whiteness of the sheet flowing around me, and there was no one to hold my hand but a nurse who didn't know my real name. I cried during the worst of it, cried out long and high, and then the doctor pulled off his gloves, the snap of latex, the whispering sound as they landed in the wastebasket, and it was over.

Afterward, I asked to see it. There wasn't much, clots of blood and a few meaty-looking pieces of membrane. While the nurse was gone, I picked up the bloody remains, wrapped them in tissue, and hid them in my jacket pocket. I rushed for the door and when the sunlight hit my face, I felt branded and exposed. I felt ugly.

When I got home, I stared at myself in the bathroom mirror. My face was ghostly and pale, as if I had used up all the years of my life. I was hot, dizzy, an infection already burning through my body as I unpacked the tissue and folded the tough pieces of membrane and small, blackish clots of blood into my hands. I held them up to my nose. They smelled of blood and earth and the secret, sullen smells between my own legs. I placed a small piece on my tongue. It tasted slippery and warm, and I swallowed without thinking.

Something warm running down my thighs, I couldn't understand where it was coming from, my head fuzzy and when I tried to punch the telephone numbers they blurred and wavered. Then a knock at my door, Deena's voice crying out my name. I pulled myself up and stumbled to the door, a trail of blood over the floor behind me. I worried how I would clean it up; I didn't want the landlady to know. Then my sister walked in the room, smelling like outside air, like night, like cigarettes.

"I'm okay," my voice brave, stubborn, but my legs shook and I was falling slowly, it seemed to last forever, the floor rising up, my eyes eager: Yes, yes. I wanted to die, but I didn't. Towels packed inside my shorts, Deena helping me down to the car. My head dizzy and powerful as I slipped in and out of dreams. I don't know where she took me, it wasn't a hospital, maybe the clinic where I had it done. Maybe it wasn't even night, maybe I just imagined that. Maybe I wasn't even bleeding, maybe she just took me for a ride afterward.

But this is what I remember: Leaning my head back on the seat as Deena drove me through the desert and I stared up at the sky. And stars, so many stars rushing up to greet me.

⁓

The first time I said it, admitted it, was at a sexual abuse support group in Tucson, up on the north side, close to the mountains. I arrived late and sat with five other women. We all looked so normal, so healthy, so nice. We signed a contract, agreed to keep everything private, that nothing we said could leak outside the group. We agreed to complete the entire program. Then we wrote out our checks. It was so normal, as if we were all at a Tupperware party.

The therapist's name was Ann or Pam or Helen, one of those nice, slightly Midwestern-sounding names that immediately conjures up cornfields and country roads and boys in ripped T-shirts hanging around gas stations. She rubbed her feet, that was the first thing I noticed, that as we told our stories, she sat with her legs folded beneath her and rubbed her feet.

I didn't go first, but I didn't go last, either. My voice trembled and shook. I gulped water, hiccupped. I was ashamed at how I sounded, my voice high-pitched, young. So much like a girl: weak, needy. I didn't cry until afterward, driving home in that cool desert night. Then I pulled over, up on River Road, and sobbed so hard I was sure I would break, my bones snapping and splintering. I didn't return. The therapist called and urged me to come back, to try again, but I told her that I couldn't, I just couldn't.

That's a lie, I went back, even though I didn't want to, even though each step toward the door of the office, such a normal, bland-looking building with a vending machine right in the doorway as if welcoming me, each step was an agony, a pain that fluttered deep in my chest, pounding along with my heartbeat.

"You keep right on walking," it sang. And I did, I walked into that room, sat down with those other women. I told my story. Every goddamned word.

That's another lie. I told my story, yes, but not every word. Some of them, a few of them, I kept for myself.

———— ✎ ————

Deena and I didn't talk to each other about what had happened to us, not then, though we would later, when we lived thousands of miles away and the phone offered us a line of safety. We couldn't talk to each other about such things, they were too raw and shameful; they hurt too much. We alluded to it, though. We both knew that the other knew, that we were bound together in shame and guilt, anger and love.

I didn't mention her weight, which had dipped down to less than ninety pounds. None of us did, not Dawn, who was a nurse, not our mother, who grudgingly supported Deena until she found a waitressing job, or Debbie, who was in graduate school back East. When we were all together, which was seldom, we played cards, almost squirming with the effort of our silence. It was so deep, this silence, so embedded inside of us that to speak, to utter one word, would have been sacrilegious.

When Deena wasn't around, my other sisters and I talked about her, worried about what we should do.

"We can't just let her starve herself to death," we said. We talked about treatment centers, counseling, medications. These options comforted us. We talked about committing Deena to a hospital, forcing her into therapy, getting our mother to cut off her funds until she agreed to seek help.

But we couldn't. We didn't have the energy. We could barely keep ourselves together. We didn't have enough left to save Deena, and so we did nothing. We offered her food and watched her starve herself. We drove her to the store to buy candy and oatmeal she would later throw up. We listened to her hysterical complaints about men who were trying to kill her and rape her, and we pressed our lips together and sighed.

All our lives Deena had been the scapegoat, the sacrificial lamb, lying up on the altar with her legs parted. Like Christ, she gave herself up for all our sins, threw up our hate and bitterness, starved our greed and disillusionments, ate our shames and secrets. She closed her eyes and waited for the knife to hit her neck, bleed her dry, not just for her, but for us, all of us.

We should have exalted her, raised her up, glorified her not for her destruction but for freeing us from our own worst intentions. But we never did. We were too young and scared and selfish. We took what we could get, and then we turned away.

I remember the only time I ever mentioned her weight. I was standing in her kitchen, in front of her opened refrigerator door, the shelves so bare and anonymous that they reminded me of a hospital room. There was nothing inside, not one hint of food, not one smudge of ketchup or drop of milk.

"You're killing yourself," I screamed. "Don't you care that you're killing yourself?"

She leaned against the windowsill and lit a cigarette.

"You're going to be dead in a couple of years, don't you care?"

She stood and stared until I dropped my eyes, as ashamed and embarrassed as if I had caught her in an intimate act: taking a shower or slowly, tenderly touching herself.

The evening before I left Arizona to move back to Alaska, Deena came to see me. I reached out and grabbed her hand and we stood in that dimming light, her grip tight, almost painful, as if she never wanted to let go.

I didn't know then that except for a few brief visits, this would be the last time I'd get to spend with Deena. She would soon marry, go back East with her new husband and I'd stay in Alaska and have a child. I didn't know that this messy, fucked-up year we shared together would be the one year I would yearn for, mourn for, expand and highlight until it became more than it was ever meant to be. I didn't know how much I'd miss Deena's dry chuckle and the familiar weight of her feet against mine as we curled up on opposite ends of the couch together, reading.

It would take over fifteen years and her death before I'd understand that I'd never gotten over the closeness we shared growing up. That of all the men I've loved and lost, all the dreams that soured and went bad, all the things I've wanted but never received, nothing has hurt as much as my first break with Deena, that jagged, brutal break that snuck up on us when we were teenagers and began to bleed, that break that was inevitable, that couldn't be stopped. Everyone I've loved, every single person, even my son, has really been Deena, a part of Deena, the way she smiled or laughed. Her haughtiness or abruptness. Her stubborn nature, her self-reliance, her chapped, mocking lips lowering against my ear and whispering, teasing:

"Cin, hey Cin, would you listen to this."

This is how I like to remember Deena: Sitting in a church together when we still lived in Tucson, both of us bored and lonely and trying to find solace in God. It was an early evening service, most of the pews filled with elderly women praying for good fortune at bingo. During the liturgy as we were kneeling and I was nodding off to the priest's words, Deena's voice suddenly filled the air.

"Through him, with him, in him," she sang, her voice strong and clear in that large room. The priest hesitated. No one else was supposed to be singing but Deena didn't stop. She refused to back down. She squared her shoulders and raised her chin.

She kept right on singing.

INTERLUDE 3

Tucson, Arizona

Twenty-five years later, I return to Tucson and it all comes back, the dust and the chaparral and night falling sudden and thick, like a blanket over my head. I sit out in the yard of the house I've sublet, breeze blowing juniper branches across my hair. It's so different here, exotic and open, the sun shadowing everything yellow and holy.

Nights the wind picks up and blows tree branches against the window. I stand out in the yard, the stars overhead, the heat lifting and the air cool, and throw back my head, give up my face to the night, the wind, the strange and dusty desert air. Sometimes I open my mouth, as if to swallow the smells, the air. I want to take it all in, I want to be consumed. It's not that I expect to be saved. It's not like that at all.

~ ⁒ ~

I walk along the dried Santa Cruz riverbed with a writer friend who used to live in Alaska. We talk of our work and our lives, our fears and hopes and pasts. I am so happy to see her again that I reach out and squeeze her hand. She names the plants we pass, the trees. She talks about her mother, about life changes.

Like Deena, this woman also struggles with anorexia and when I hug her, she is so thin, her bones so light, I'm afraid she might snap. She doesn't, though. She is stronger than my sister. She isn't afraid to make herself vulnerable. This was Deena's failing, and mine too. For years, I fought to appear stronger than I was until I became aloof and distant, afraid to ask for help.

A year ago, this woman tried to kill herself. I went to visit her in the hospital, after they moved her to the psych ward, and she looked small and alone yet defiant. I like that she looked defiant.

Now she is tanned and writing again. She takes spiritual classes, submits her work to prestigious literary magazines. I love her, I don't know why. She reminds me of Deena, the good and soft parts of Deena that I knew growing up.

Is that selfish? I don't give a damn. I want this woman to eat, to nourish herself. I want her to make it. I want her to do it for Deena.

In the desert, the rain falls like a gift, not the way it falls in Alaska, heavy and sullen, unapologetic. In the desert, the rain falls like music, like a song, and hours after it stops and the chaparral dries off and the air becomes dusty and dry again, you can still hear it in the back of your mind, the way a favorite song plays over and over, the melody caught in your throat, and so even as you speak, you can feel it against your tongue, taste it around the curve of your vowels: Rain, rain. Rain.

Years ago, after writing a newspaper story on green funerals, I made out my funeral plans and sent them to my youngest sister. I wrote that I wanted to be cremated, that I didn't want a service. I wanted to be burned, not buried. Sometimes, though, I think of the earth and how cool the dirt feels against my fingers. I think of the mountains and the inlet, the warm rocks in the desert canyons, and I want to return there, I want to be buried in a shallow grave on the south side of a mountain, in the sunlight. I want animals roaming the ground that covers me. I want my bones weathered smooth as driftwood.

This won't happen, though. I'll die, hopefully not for a long time, and I'll be cremated, my ashes scattered in the mountains and along the beach during high tide.

It's scary, isn't it, to think of death, of no longer existing. How is it possible that we can no longer exist?

FEEDING

~~⚬~~

Words from the Dead

She might have escaped had she bothered to try, but she couldn't think of anywhere to go.

—the last page of Deena's notebook

Anchorage, Alaska

I had been expecting the call for years but when it finally came, the experience was blurry and vague, almost surreal. I groped around the floor for the phone, my mind fuzzy, the living room tinted with the bluish light of an Alaska morning, a light that speaks of dimming but not darkness, of days stretching out stubborn and plentiful. It's easy to feel invincible on such days, easy to believe that the sun and light will go on forever.

The window was open, that's what I remember, and the way the air smelled, damp and silty from the inlet. I don't know if a raven cooed right when I picked up the phone, but it should have, I should have heard the news accompanied by that deep-throated, mournful cry.

My mother was the one who said it, told me that Deena had died. "She's gone," that's how she put it. There was more, of course, details and times, funeral arrangements, plane fares, and telephone numbers. I huddled on the couch, the dog at my feet, the cat staring from the desk. I stayed like that for hours, until my son ran in from outside, his long legs flashing beneath shorts.

"Mom!" he shouted, not knowing or caring about my grief. "Mom, I'm hungry."

I got up and made grilled cheese sandwiches, I buttered the bread, the cheese melting in fat strips down the sides. I set out plates, napkins, glasses of lemonade. I sat down at our small table, and I watched my son eat.

─ ✑ ─

She was driving a taxi, wearing a pink shirt, such a hopeful pink. I imagine her buttoning it early that evening, one of those impatient motions we never notice, the simple miracle of our fingers moving buttons through small holes. Pulling on her pants, tying her shoes. Her blood, ah, her blood still flowing through her veins.

It happened after a few hours, when it was still early in her shift. Maybe she worried about money, making money, she never had enough money, it was always such a struggle. Or maybe not. Maybe she noticed the sky, the stars, the moon.

This is what I like to think: that when the pains first came, she was staring up at the sky.

A spring afternoon years and years before this happened, driving up to Alaska with a man I would later leave. The Yukon still covered with snow but there were patches of green, places we stopped where the spruce trees whispered and sighed. Wind wild in my hair. We camped at Destruction Bay, waves pounding the shore with an energy that pulsed my veins until I ran back and forth, back and forth, I couldn't stop.

Night came softly, weaving in through the daylight so that it was like falling asleep, the way the light slowly closed its eyes and darkness took over, a dim, silver darkness that fell over my shoulders and erased everything. No lights, no houses, the moon arching so low and fat across the sky it looked as if I could reach it with my hand.

So far north, the air is more relaxed, the trees greener, the mountains steeper and wiser. You can lose yourself in a place like this. You can let down your defenses, stop running. You can finally stay still.

The last time I saw Deena was the year I took my son back and we all met on the farm. Deena was strange, childish, talking in a high-pitched voice. Plaintive, whining, begging for attention. It was almost as if she were competing with my son for cuteness, for the small morsels of attention and love left over in our hardened hearts. She didn't know how to act any other way. Alone so much, she must have withdrawn into a world of her own making. Secretive. Sly. Needy.

When there were just the three of us, she was different. We walked through the fields, Deena, my son, and I, and I held her hand, her fingers clasping mine tightly, almost painfully, with the desperation of someone who hasn't been touched in a long time. We walked up the path, barely visible anymore, but we knew it, we could have found it anywhere.

I pointed out things to my son: the old pond, the trees we used to climb. Everything was overgrown, so many wild and stubborn weeds, many higher than our heads. It pleased me, the way weeds had obliterated the past, our memories replaced by ragweed and dandelion and scrub brush. Though of course we were still there, we would always be there, hidden inside those trees and dark, shady places. Our little girl legs running and jumping, our small, hopeful arms waving and pushing. The smells and sounds of the cows. The dog running ahead. It was a paradise, once. Our own little Eden. Of course, we fell. We fell hard and flat, with no one to catch us.

Still, it was glorious. Even our misery was sweet. Humid, like a fly droning around your ear. I used to pick handfuls of dirt, smear it across my mouth, picking up pieces with my tongue and slowly swallowing: sweet grass, alfalfa, clover so rich my eyes watered.

─୨୧─

Angel, Jake calls to me in the dark, the moon shining across his mouth. *Angel, my sweet, sweet angel.*

─୨୧─

I remember Jake's voice over the phone the day after Deena died. I lay on the couch, a Sandra Bullock movie playing over and over and behind it his voice, low and soft and deep. I grabbed it, held on tight. I barely knew him then, he was some-one from work, someone I traded books with and talked to in the newsroom on Sundays when I wrote the obituaries and needed a break from all that death. He was nobody; I wasn't sure of his last name. But after that phone call, I saw him differently, almost as if an aura hung around him.

The first time he kissed me, his breath tasted of sleep and a lingering of garlic from the spaghetti he'd eaten the night before. I hesitated for a moment, thinking of all those childhood suppers, the smell of dandelions and hay drifting through the open windows, all that meat thick and heavy on the platters, mashed potatoes and gravy and milk waiting to coat my tongue and throat with an awful furry thickness. I thought of all this. Then I closed my eyes, pressed my lips against his. I swallowed his tastes.

I wonder if Deena thought of me as she was dying, of our mother, of home. The way the mud in the creek squished between our toes when we chased the cows in the summers. We loved that creek, loved that mud. We used to smear it over our faces and wait for it to dry, moving our chins to feel it crack.

We ate that mud sometimes, overcome by the heat and the languor of the afternoons, the slow, steady buzz of insects. We never minded the cow pies littering the banks, or the flies, or when the cows wandered and pushed their way past us. We stood up to our knees in water, surrounded by the cows' hot and smelly hides.

I like to think that death freed Deena, left her happy and wild, the way she used to be. Wings tattered and dirty, halo covered with burrs. An angel praying with filthy, chapped hands.

As soon as I heard that Deena had died, I called people: the medical examiner, the hospital, the taxi company where she had worked. I babbled on incoherently. Some of them hung up on me and I had to call them over and over to make them understand who I was and what I wanted: A tiny piece of my sister. Her last words or motions. The color of her shirt.

Finally, I got in touch with her landlady. She hadn't known Deena long, she said. She had just taken over the building a few months before. Her voice fast as if she were nervous talking about this woman who had died and left her things in her house. As if I might accuse her, make it her fault.

"We didn't talk much but she seemed nice," she said. "She didn't want no trouble."

I could hear that there was something she wasn't telling me, so I waited.

"Always had that dog with her. She just loved that dog, you could see. Loved it to pieces."

I asked her about Deena's things, told her not to throw anything away, that someone would be down to collect them. Deena, she finally told me in an apologetic voice, was behind on the rent.

"Don't know who she was yelling at that night," she said. "Sounded like an ugly fight. It went on and on."

She was screaming, the landlady said, screaming at the top of her lungs, screaming for a long, long time.

"Didn't anyone do anything?" I said, my voice rising in anger. "Call the cops? Go check on her?"

"She seemed so proud," the landlady said. "We just didn't think it was right."

After a few feigned formalities, we hung up. That's the last time I ever talked with that woman, though my mother called her a few times after that, unable to let go since she was the last link to Deena.

The phone call bothered me for years, still bothers me. Not the call but the knowledge: That Deena was mad the night before she died. Crazy and screaming at someone who wasn't there. Who did she think she saw, what demons did she imagine she fought? Whatever it was, I hope she put up a good fight, even if it was all in her head. I hope she cried and screamed and pounded her fists against the floor until they were bloody and scraped. I hope she yelled and fumed and got it all out, purified herself from the stench of her own fears.

We are all mad inside of our heads, mad with our memories and sins, our rages, our regrets and shames and false penances. Maybe Deena was sick of hiding, maybe she needed to let it all out, every fucking piece of what she was feeling, and it overwhelmed her. It drove her crazy.

Or maybe that last night she was levelheaded, clear, her mind at peace. Maybe she drove her taxicab around with the calm assurance of the redeemed. Someone at the taxi company told me that the passengers she had with her at the time believe Deena saved their lives, and that as soon as the pains hit, she yelled "Whoa, there," and steered the car safely over the side of the road before slumping across the steering wheel.

We used to say those words back on the farm, not when riding horses, because Deena didn't like to ride, but as we were running through the fields.

"Whoa," we shouted when we did something silly, stepped in a cow pie or tripped and fell in the creek. Teasing, rolling our eyes as we pulled ourselves up, wiped off the blood, falling against each other and shouting out, our voices never in time so it sounded like an echo.

"Whoa, there. Whhhooooaaa there."

Sometimes I cry in Jake's arms. He doesn't ask me what is wrong, he doesn't say anything. He just holds me there, with his arms and his legs.

There, like that.

Just like that.

~∾~

The day of Deena's funeral was sunny, the sky almost clear, even though it had sprinkled in the morning. But that's another lie. I can't remember if it was sunny, I can't remember the sky at all. Maybe it was overcast, dim clouds spreading in from the lake. I didn't look up at the sky, didn't even realize there was a sky, because I was driving to the funeral home early in the morning to dress my sister's body and nothing made fucking sense.

I met the funeral director in the parking lot, the same funeral home where my father had been laid out so many years before. The director had on sandals and shorts, casual wear since it was early and the office hadn't yet opened. He led me down the back stairs, ordinary cement stairs that led down into the basement, and stopped in front of the door, a wooden door; it could have been the door to a bedroom or bathroom except for the smells hiding behind it: thick and persuasive, ugly. The door opened slowly.

There was Deena, up on a table, a white sheet pulled from her shoulders to her ankles, one foot stubbornly poking out. The funeral director touched my shoulder, said that if I needed anything to call; there was a phone hanging on the wall. Then he left. I stood in that quiet and bare room; I stood with the body of my dead sister. My head swirled and I reached out, clutched the corner of the table. I couldn't breathe.

A white plastic bodysuit covered her upper body. It looked like one of those old-fashioned swimsuits from the twenties, with bloomers attached to the legs. This, according to the funeral director, was to keep fluids from draining through. I resented this suit, and the noise it made when I leaned down to touch Deena's arm and accidently nudged a corner. It sounded like paper towels crinkling in the bathroom or a grocery sack being folded and shoved away in the cupboard. Leftover noises from the things we don't want to see.

Her legs were tanned, her calves unnaturally puffed and rubbery from the embalming fluid. I ran my hand over her knee, which was thicker, more substantial than it had been in life. Tiny hairs itched my palm and suddenly this seemed the worst thing, that my sister had died without a chance to shave her legs. That she had no way of knowing, dressing for work that evening, that her heart would finally give out, that she would be rushed to the hospital without the chance of doing or saying the things we all know, in the backs of our minds, we would do and say to prepare for our own death.

I began to dress her. I lifted her hips and it was dreadful how awkward her body was, how motionless it remained. I wanted to smack and shake her: Wake up! Instead I struggled with the underpants, silk twisting against my fingers, the bodysuit crinkling as I pulled it up to her waist and smoothed down the leg. Then I moved down to the end of the table and pulled on thick socks. Her toenails were long and ragged, and I thought of dressing my son when he was small, his chubby feet, his round and domed belly, and how his skin smelled of milk and grass.

I wrapped my hand around her ankle. The skin was cold and hideous. Still, I couldn't stop touching her. I ran my hands over her collarbone, her knee, my fingers lingering. I tugged the last wrinkles out of the dress and combed her hair with my fingers. She didn't look the way I expected. I had imagined making her beautiful, but she wasn't. She was dead and cold. She wasn't my sister. She had nothing to do with my sister. Still, I couldn't leave. I stood by the table, clutching my hands around her arm.

I stood there a long, long time.

During the funeral service, we focused on my ten-year-old son. The only child, the last of the blood. Oh, the pressure, the expectations; how his thin, pale shoulders drooped under the attentions. He was doomed to fail us all.

This is what he will do: he will fail us, and I will applaud him.

Be anything, I whisper to him as he sleeps. Be a mechanic, a janitor. A bus driver. Forget school and offices and sitting behind a computer. Travel! Grow your hair long! Hitchhike through Europe and dance with girls with thick, peasant ankles.

I hope he marries someone unconventional, someone with a wild heart and a warm smile. I hope he grows potatoes and knows the pleasure of dirt beneath his fingernails.

This is what I wish for him: the happiness, the pure, uncompromising joy of the smell of damp grass.

After Deena died, I started to cut myself again. I wanted to bleed, feel blood flow over my skin. It wasn't that I wanted to hurt myself so much as I couldn't stand not hurting. The pain was so deep and urgent.

I did this late at night, sitting in the empty bathtub, a pink disposable razor in my hand. A woman's razor, curved to fit my palm. It was comforting, that plastic, and the way it hurt as I sliced into my ankle or arm or chest. I made small cuts, a few inches in diameter, and then worked the blade deep inside, pushing and pressing, eyes watering, teeth biting down on my lip.

The blood came slowly at first, a few drops and then more and more. I sat there, blood trickling down my breasts or across my foot, and I rocked back and forth, crying and moaning, gasping. Some nights I stuck a washcloth in my mouth and screamed, over and over, blood forming puddles at my feet. Once I smeared it over my face, my lips, rubbed it into the soft, pink spaces above my teeth. Marked, branded. It was the only thing that made me feel better.

Jake knows about the stars, though I've never asked him. I like knowing that in his head, he can name things: constellations, galaxies. Though I prefer to stay in the dark. This way, when I look up in the sky, I see lights, shadows, the round flicker of a moon. Like ancient people staring up at the sky, that wonder, that fear. That mystery.

No one went down to Florida to retrieve Deena's things. A dishonor, a snub, the kind of slight that shouldn't be made. She deserved that much, at least. That someone she knew, someone who loved her would be the one to go through her private things: her toothbrush, her underwear. Her towels. Old maxi pads, razors, magazines.

I made plans, flying in from Alaska to the farm and then on to Florida—almost two days' worth of traveling. I imagined walking into her small apartment, folding her clothes, packing up her books, her pictures. Matching her socks and running my hands over the frayed elastic of her underpants. Everything smelling of smoke. Old Diet Pepsi cans filling the trash. The refrigerator empty and bare, the shelves not even dirty. This is what I expected. But in the end, I didn't go. I was too afraid. I didn't know what to do with my son. Take him to that house of death, of loss, where my sister's few things littered the floor like remains of a war? Or leave him back at the house where I grew up, in that country darkness with no sounds but the crickets and the hay swaying ripe in the fields, the sounds of footsteps shuffling up the hallway; in that bedroom of all my broken dreams?

A year before she died, Deena called and made me promise
that I would never leave my son alone in that house. The call
was unexpected. By then, she rarely contacted any of us. I was
in the middle of cooking dinner; I barely listened.

"No matter what," she said. "Promise?"

I shrugged, promised. I didn't see the point, since he would
never travel across the country alone. I promised, gave my
word as I stirred spaghetti sauce, opened the oven to check
the biscuits. Air hot against my face, the smell of rising yeast. I
nodded, promised, worried about whether I had remembered to
buy butter and if my son had brought home his math homework.

We talked for a while longer, hung up. And I didn't think of
it until after she died and I considered leaving my son in that
house as I flew down to Florida to box up my sister's stuff.

"Promise," her voice not questioning but challenging.
Definite, almost angry. Almost mocking, as if she knew I might
betray her.

If she were alive, she would have told me not to bother, that
things were just things. To just burn everything, get rid of it all.

But I wanted something: her clothes, her smells. I wanted
to make a quilt of her shirts, know what brand of toothpaste
she used. I wanted to wash my face with her washcloths, pee
in her toilet, feel my bare feet walk over her bathroom floor in
the middle of the night. I wanted the intimacy of her life, the
last few lingering tidbits.

Instead I stayed at the farm with my son, roaming through
the fields at night, crying, screaming out her name. My feet
bare, the soles bloodied by morning. I crept through the yard
and down into the fields, weeds higher than my waist, sharp
stabs of stone beneath my feet. I welcomed each pain. I wanted
to hurt, to bleed. I wanted to pay for this death, this betrayal.

Sometimes, running through those tall weeds, I could feel
her behind me, and I slipped through time until I was a child
again, thin and stubborn and following the flash of her white
shirt, both of our voices high with the feel of summer and the

steady weight of our legs carrying us over hills and through the cold, damp mud alongside the creek.

The first time I ate dinner with Jake, I was self-conscious. We sat at a small table across from each other. The room was very bright, the light coming in the large windows behind us. I felt ugly, exposed. I fidgeted, I couldn't keep still.

He made burritos, salad. He had hot sauce, a light dressing. I was afraid he would see my mouth while I ate, afraid of how it looked, hungry and ugly, as if all my appetites would be revealed: all my loneliness and longings, my angers and fears and awful, aching neediness. I was afraid that I would disgust him.

But I ate. I made myself eat. I talked and ate, and really, it was easier than I thought. Before I knew it, the burrito was gone and so was the salad. I wiped my lips with my napkin, got up to put my plate in the kitchen.

"Are you still hungry?" he asked. "Do you want more?"

I was. I did. I had more.

Deena and I were good at lying, words slipping from our tongues easily, effortlessly. Good Catholic girls, we went to confession each week, standing with our hands folded, our cotton dresses ironed without a crease. White socks, patent leather shoes, ribbons in our hair. Clean and nice; holy.

Still, we never confessed to the priest our deepest, truest sins. Not the things that were done to us, or even the things men made us do. Our sins were worse: the things we wanted, the things we desired. We held these secrets tight to our chests, kept them in the dark, where they festered and grew dank. For years I kept my hand over my mouth when I spoke to people in nice clothes and city haircuts, people who spoke in educated speech and lived in homes without secrets. I kept my hand over my mouth, spoke briefly and then turned away, sure that they would be able to smell the stink coming out of my mouth. The ugly, fetid smell of my lies.

When I was pregnant with my son, Deena sent me boxes of baby clothes, little outfits of blue and green, teddy bears that played music, bibs with ducks marching bravely across them. I wept, unfolding those clothes that my sister had packed so carefully. There was so much hope inside each one, so much desire, so much raw, anguished love. I knew that she would never have children. With her weight so low (though she insisted over the phone that she was eating, that she was quite healthy, that she was working two jobs and running and riding her bike every night), I wondered if she was even able to get pregnant, if she still had her period, that reassuring rush of blood. I never asked, though. We rarely talked about our bodies.

I was very sick during my pregnancy, a morning sickness that lingered the entire nine months. I was unable to work, unable, some days, to walk to the bathroom without holding my palms out flat against the walls. I went to doctors and specialists and no one could find anything wrong. I was healthy, they insisted. Really, there was nothing wrong with me. But still I was sick, so sick, and finally I had to go on welfare, a shame so great that I often couldn't cash the check. I left it squatting on the dresser, where it mocked me each time I walked into the room.

Deena sent me boxes filled with cards and coupons and clothes. A pair of overalls, soft denim, the only nice thing I had to wear. She sent me money also, and I used this for soaps and lotions, which I rubbed over my round belly, the skin stretched tight around the curved ache of my son's arms and legs. It was a miracle, it made my hands shake to think what I had done, the enormity of my actions, how one night with a man

I barely knew could end up with this, could give me this. It was something I never shared with Deena, couldn't possibly put into words, my fear and awe along with the horrible pregnancy hunger, an all-consuming hunger that caused me to eat potato salad in the middle of the night, eating with my bare hands because I was too impatient to look for a clean spoon. Scooping it up with my fingers, sticking it in my mouth, and often I groaned, sitting back against the couch cushions, and what I thought to myself was: Yes, ah, sweet Jesus, yes.

I like to take Jake in my mouth after we make love. He is soft and salty, and I lick off all his tastes.

Sometimes I weep doing this. He is so soft, he smells so good. I lay my head against his thigh, close my eyes. I imagine sleeping like this, with him still in my mouth. It feels so safe.

After Deena died, I began to see a therapist again, a short-term counselor designed for quick fixes without those deep, agonizing dives into the past. This one believed in jogging straight through, no stopping when the pain hits, just breathe deep and lift your knees and keep on going. So that's what I did, I ran through my life, slowing down here and there to stretch the kinks out of my legs. It was refreshing, this approach; I was used to digging down deep and stalling inside my misery.

This therapist said it wasn't my fault, that Deena was crazy, that there was nothing I could have done. He had a receding hairline, and a large, round forehead that I found strangely compelling. I wondered if he had a family, children, if he was gay. If he liked to read poetry or ride a bike along the coastal trail and would I ever pass him, dear sweet God, on the hiking trails or while swimming at one of the lakes?

Week after week I sat in that office surrounded by pillows, though maybe there weren't really pillows there, maybe I am just adding them to soften the picture, but I sat there, in my newspaper work clothes, dresses and skirts, my professional costume, I sat there and I felt like a period, a comma, something waiting for a pause.

Finally, I quit going. I missed an appointment, then another. I was feeling better, I lied. I was okay now, it was nothing. I was over it.

She comes to me in my dreams sometimes, a blessing, the way the dead can return to us and how much dearer they are, for even during the dream, that short amount of time when we are sleeping and lost to our thoughts, even then we know to be thankful.

Nine months after Deena dies, I think that I am pregnant. An impossibility, since Jake has had a vasectomy. Still, as my period grows later and later, as my breasts swell so heavy that they ache each night as I take off my bra, I begin to wonder. At first I am sick with dread, hunched over the toilet with feigned morning sickness. I don't want another child. I am too old, too poor; there are too many things I would have to give up.

Two days later, when my period is almost four weeks late, I am driving home and blinded by the sun. For a moment I am helpless, unable to see, not sure if I am swerving or still on the road. In that a moment, barely a second, so short it is less than a blink, it suddenly strikes me that I am carrying my sister's child, the one she was meant to have if only her life had been different.

The thought is sobering, immense. My hands shake, my teeth chatter. I pull off on the side of the road and park in front of a tire store, the blue and yellow sign so cheerful and vague it is like a pat on the back. I suck in my breath. Close my eyes. And is that when I begin to hope, foolishly, desperately?

It is, I do. Foolish, this hope, this sly, clever hope, and the way it wraps around my mind, teasing me toward a place I have no wish to follow. But of course, I do. I begin to hope, silently, hands folded as if in prayer. And I am praying, rashly, foolishly. I even get down on my knees later that night, bowing in front of the couch in the summer twilight, fingers clasped, teeth biting my lip as I grope to remember the old words.

"Our Father, Hail Mary . . . ." The words stumble out of my lips like something cracked and rusted, but I don't care about words, or even what they're supposed to mean. What I want is impossible, hopeless, a doomed, suffering miracle. I want my sister back, now, right now. I want her to walk through the living room, a cigarette cocked in her mouth. I want to see the reassuring curve of her neck as she leans down over a book.

If I can't have this, I want something else, something to take her place. A child.

It's ugly, hideous, almost obscene, the things we pray and hope for. The things we know we can't have.

─ ⟋ ─

I remember the first time I tried to write, I was eleven and it was summer and I hunched over a sheet of paper, a pen in my hand, splotches over the page, and suddenly words came out, I don't know where they came from. It was like magic, how they opened inside my head. It was like something hatching or being born.

I can't remember what I wrote. Perhaps it was a poem or maybe a song. But I still recall the feeling: it was like being free, like how I would feel when I lost my virginity years later, that flap of skin finally broken, opening me up to something vast and unmentionable, something I could neither turn away from nor control. Something that I wouldn't, couldn't refuse.

~ ༠ᕊ ~

I like to take a bath in Jake's house while he cooks for me. I lie in his bathtub, the water hot and soapy as I read magazines and novels, and his bathroom is nice, sensual and orderly, very clean but not bare. The kind of room where every corner glints with possibilities. I always think about sex when I'm in his bathroom. Not sex, but bodies: his body, mine. The way we look and smell and touch. His bathroom makes me want to linger, though when we are together, we can't linger, we just can't, we want each other too much.

The kitchen is right behind the bathroom so I can hear pots clang, cupboards open and close, the sound of the knife on the chopping block. I lie back, close my eyes, imagine his hands over me, imagine doing it on the counter with onion and garlic sticking to my ass. Sometimes I touch myself, but usually I don't. The water is warm and flows against me. I don't want to come. I want to wait.

When the smells start seeping in, I imagine him moving around. I know how he moves, carefully, gracefully, with little wasted motion. His back straight, but his arms fluid. He wears rubber flip-flop slippers, something I find ridiculous yet endearing. His hair is short and I lie there, imagining licking his neck.

Instead I stay in the bathtub until the water cools. Then I get out, dry off. Put my clothes back on. Sometimes I stare at myself in his mirror and wonder how he sees me. As a thin, easily excited woman with blond streaks through her hair and arms that wave as she talks? As someone who walks with long, athletic strides and often feels trapped indoors?

The bathroom is always steamy when I leave it, and for a moment the hallway feels cold. Then I go out in the kitchen, sit down. We eat. And no matter how good it is, nothing compares to lying in a hot bath knowing someone is out in the kitchen cooking for me.

———— ✺ ————

We burned her, this was my idea. I don't even know if she would have wanted it. She was afraid of so many things, fire was probably one of them. But it was either that or the cemetery plot at home, beside our father, in that shaded place by the lake, smells of damp air, and in the summer, humid and still, with that expectation of motion, of waiting. There could be worse places to lay down your bones, surrounded there by family: grandmothers and grandfathers, Italian and Irish relatives, on separate sides of the cemetery, hot blood and cold blood mixed inside our veins until we wished longed couldn't breathe until we escaped.

But sweetie, you said, I promised, you wanted nothing to do with it there, you said, you told me, so I did, and how do I know if it was a good thing or a bad thing? I told them, I insisted that they not leave you back there, and remember how we longed dreamed fought to escape? Wandering, we didn't know and didn't want to know, but what we longed for, secretly, fearfully, what we longed for was somewhere, anywhere, someplace to kick up and just be ourselves, our goddamned flawed awful selfish selves.

Burn her, I said, because I knew that fire purifies and I wanted your bones burned clean. I didn't say it that way, but that's what I meant. Fire, orange and yellow flames, and remember how fascinated we were, lighting matches in the pastures, down by the creek, and the time the barn caught on fire, the hay too green, flames sputtering, though they caught it in time, the wood didn't even catch, and were you as disappointed as me? Did you want to see it burn, all of it, every damned acre inch plot of that land, burning and scorching, all of our lies and betrayals covered with ash?

Remember that day, the day a neighbor's barn burned and we stood out there, the flames stretching to the sky, the heat almost searing our faces, everyone was there, it was like a celebration, a sick, ugly, gut-churning festival, and I was scared, Jesus lord I was so scared, and I looked over at you, your eyes open, your face surprised and pure, and I thought, I saw, your face your eyes, and I thought: This is what it looks like to be holy.

So I did it, sweetie girl. I made you glow.

"What's the worst thing you've ever done?" I ask Jake. We're lying in his bed, the mountains outside the window. It's cool in the room, the window open, the sounds of the wind and the trees behind my voice. He pauses for a long time. I lie naked beside him, not touching, waiting.

When he finally speaks, his voice is strained: this is hard for him. I move closer, the heat of his chest against my shoulder, and I suck in my breath, waiting. I don't know what I expect, the usual betrayals, the fucking around on someone, the leaving when someone needed him, the petty, ugly things we all do to each other. But it isn't even that; he isn't even capable of that. What he tells me is so bland, so inconsequential, so safe and harmless that I almost sneer, my face pressed against those white sheets.

Listening to him tell his story, halting, as if he's never told anyone before, I almost laugh, I almost snort: This, I want to scream in hysterical laughter, this is it, this is the best you can come up with?

It's as if he is giving me something, offering me his own worst self, and yet how can I reach out and take it when my own sins are so much darker and malevolent, when they have to do with blood and pain, words so sharp they could cut skin? I want to collapse against his chest, crying it all out. But I remain silent.

∽✥∾

When he was small, I used to lick my son's hair, I don't know why. Picking him up after he fell asleep and carrying him to his room, and then leaning down and kissing his head. My tongue stealing out, burrowing down inside his hair, that grainy softness, that taste of grass and woods and milk.

It was good, pure. It tasted like rain.

∽✥∾

I don't know what love is: What is love? Nothing like the songs or the movies. Love burrows through your bones. It makes you bleed. It makes you ache. It's the worst of anything.

I loved Deena, but I didn't always like her. Who says we have to like the people we love, who says we get to have that choice, that luxury? How many people are that goddamned lucky?

∽✥∾

A friend and I talk about betrayals, family betrayals, the way a word or phrase can float up from childhood and paralyze us. We are both successful, we both have jobs, children, lovers, money in the bank. Yet we both still fear the past, the way it can catch us unaware, bind us, wrap us in and hold us tight.

We become weepy, talking like this. We wipe our eyes, clear our throats, laugh uncomfortably. Then we eat. It's the only thing left to do. We buy muffins at the coffee counter, stand there in the hallway, and shove them into our mouths. We take large bites, pieces falling down our chins and hitting the floor.

When I look over at her, she has her head back, her eyes closed, it almost looks as if she is praying, but she is just eating, we are both eating. Brown sugar against our tongues, and the way the crumbs stick to the roofs of our mouths. Heavenly, sometimes, this eating.

～♻～

I tell Jake about swimming, about the way it feels, my body floating through that clear water, the bottom of the pool so blue it is like a miracle. I am so happy, swimming, my body free, my mind able to wander. I don't have to talk or listen or please anyone. I wonder, I ask him, if that is how it feels to die.

Probably, he says.

You think?

Dying is probably a beautiful thing.

I am ready to protest but then think of sleeping, when I am so tired I can't keep my eyes focused and when I finally close them, that moment of unexpected fear, and then my body taking over, diving down deeper and deeper, and really, it is like swimming, my mind kicking and stroking until I almost hit bottom.

Maybe, I finally say. Maybe it is.

～♻～

Deena wanted me to make it. She wanted to make it too, at one point. Or maybe she never did. Maybe she wanted to sink down and stay there like a child, waiting for someone to step in and take care of her. Rescue her.

She wanted me to write, publish a book. Write a story, not necessarily her story or mine, but someone's. It was important to her that I do this, prove that there were still things to be salvaged, or maybe that's another lie, maybe it's always been me, only me. Maybe I'm doing this all for myself.

Sometimes at night I go into my son's room and put eczema cream on his back. He sleeps with the blankets pulled up to his chin, small hands folded in front of his belly. I lift the covers off and he makes little animal whimpering noises, grabs blindly for the quilt. He is so defenseless, sleeping. So beautiful and warm and defenseless. I pull up his shirt, spread the cream around his back, talk to him. I tell him about the way the trees looked when I walked the dog, or how proud I am of his spelling test. Then I pull his shirt back down, tuck the blankets back beneath his chin and walk out.

By then, I am often almost shaking with anger. Because I can't help thinking of myself sleeping like that, so small and vulnerable, and how I was pulled up from sleep with those rough, ugly hands.

"How dare he!" I say, and the anger is hard and pure inside me. "How fucking dare he!" My foot pounding the floor, my fingernails biting my palm until my anger becomes a battle cry, a psalm, a holy prayer.

I feed on it, and in some strange, unexplainable way, it keeps me going.

I didn't always like being around Deena. It was like wading through mud in a pair of good shoes, and how you must always look down to try and avoid the puddles. You miss the scenery, when you're looking down. I spent so much time trying to walk over areas of conflict that I didn't hear what she was saying. I heard the words but didn't understand what was hidden behind them. I didn't want to know. I was scared, and weak, and this is something that I will always regret, always dislike myself for.

The last time she called, she begged me to come down to where she was living in Florida. She had left her husband a few years before and, more recently, a man in New Mexico. "Get a plane ticket and come now," she said. "I'm in trouble."

People were after her, she said, the FBI, the CIA, the Feds. They had implanted a microchip in her head and were carrying out experiments on her, hideous and unmentionable things. They did this late at night, from a helicopter overhead. They were killing her, she said; she could hardly stand the pain.

It's strange, isn't it, how we all listened for so many years and did nothing. It's as if silence and secrecy were so ingrained in us that when we finally needed to speak, we couldn't find the words. We didn't know the words.

I tried, though, and more than once, my voice shaking, my words quavering. I suggested a therapist, medication, but she laughed, a harsh laugh followed by a drag on her cigarette. I could hear her inhaling during the pause.

"Oh, for heaven's sakes," she said, she was always saying. "You act like I'm all fucked up or something." Another laugh, another drag on her cigarette. And then she changed the subject and talked about her dog, the book she was reading, the way the beach looked in the evening when the sun set. She sounded like herself again and so I relaxed, eased up, though still I held the receiver tight against my ear, my wrist muscles aching from the strain.

She'd call back a few weeks or a few months later, crazy again, begging me to come down, to leave my job, leave my son with a neighbor, to come down right now because they were after her and she didn't have much time left.

Sometimes I'd agree. I'd arrange time off from my job, make plane reservations, arrange for a friend to watch my son, but when I called Deena to tell her when I was coming, she wouldn't pick up. I'd leave message and message begging for her to please, please call. I wouldn't hear from her again for months. When she finally called back, her voice would be cheerful and light, as if she hadn't a care in the world.

When I went back to northern Pennsylvania the summer after Deena died, I went through her backpack, the one that had been with her when she died. We both carried backpacks, scorning purses, myself because I hate feeling prissy, my sister because she carried around so much stuff. It was her security, this stuff, I know because I often do the same thing, surround myself with objects to give me the feeling of being alive, important, someone who matters.

I was sitting at the kitchen table when my mother handed me the pack. Then she sat down beside me and waited. My son was off somewhere, out in the yard or playing games in the living room. The pack was a dark green, a color that looked like Deena: somber, serious, not one to easily reveal itself. I reached inside impatiently, angrily, because my mother should have done this last year, gone through my sister's things, sorting out what to keep and what to throw out or give away. But she had saved it for me. She couldn't do it, she told me, she just couldn't bring herself to do it.

Deena would have understood my anger, she often felt it herself, that absence of something solid to lean on, no weight beneath our feet. Maybe that's why she tried so hard to lose weight, maybe she wanted to be smaller, take up less room, less notice.

I stuck my hand inside and began unloading items: A pair of sunglasses. Her checkbook, no money, the balance overdrawn, her handwriting small and precise, columns of numbers running across the page. Pens and loose paper. Her teeth, an upper bridge in a plastic Ziploc bag. Another Ziploc bag filled with photographs, many of my son. An address book. A notebook. Eight pages of lined notebook paper filled with looped, messy writing. Old business cards, flyers, pages from books. A comb. A keyring with nothing on it. I threw most of it away, talking normally with my mother, as if this were the easiest thing in the world. I wanted to yell and scream, cry, wail out my grief, but of course we were not that kind of family. I was controlled, bitter, resentful. I hated my mother, my sister, myself, all of us, for having to do this, for this ugly green backpack, for my sister's cheap things, for the checkbook with no money, her taxi log showing that she owed more than she had made. I hated it, hated us and it and everything in that whole goddamned kitchen.

Dear sweet Christ, Deena, what did you do, where did you go, what blind spaces inside your mind did you escape to? Was it better, living like that, feeling those pains and fears? Were they better than the real ones, the ones that festered and scabbed and bled all around you, all of us?

Sister, sweetie, honey: Did you, could you, were you
did you ever, those last few moments or seconds
could you, did you let yourself see, feel, touch
beauty?

—ɔᴄ—

I dream that my son and I are hiking up the side of a mountain. Suddenly, two moose step into our path.

"Get back!" I warn my son, and he steps out of the path. But a moose kicks and lets loose a flood of small, round rocks the size of shot put balls. This starts an avalanche, and I grab my son but can't hold him. He slips out of my grasp.

Seconds later it is over, and I start digging through the rocks, an impossible task, the side of the hill is covered, thousands, maybe millions of identically shaped rocks. I dig and throw, dig and throw, searching for my son. I know he is down there somewhere. Other people appear and help, but they soon stop.

"There's no way he could still be alive," they tell me, but I go right on digging. I refuse to leave him alone in that cold, rocky place.

When I tell this dream to a friend, I cry and cry, I can't stop. She tells me that it was myself I was looking for, the lost child inside myself. This makes me sob even harder. But even as I am crying, part of me is back on the side of that mountain. Still digging.

～♒～

A few years after Deena died, I returned to the farm and stole her ashes. I didn't take all of them, though that was my intention. I left some, not a lot, but some. This had nothing to do with fear, or bravery, or trying to be good, the way I tried so hard to be good growing up. This had to do with love.

I snuck into that room, that extra room on the far side of the house where my sisters and I used to sleep, now fixed up with my mother's computer and puzzles, her sewing machine and plants. I did this in the morning, in the full light of the sun. I didn't ask, I simply reached in and poured out three plastic baggies. My mother stood in the doorway, wringing her hands and asking, begging me not to take all of it. She needed it, she said, in that room; she needed the company. A cold, hard spark of anger rose in me and I wanted to stand up, fling the ashes across the room, scream: Where were you when Deena was still alive? But I didn't. I kept pouring. I had no choice, I had promised Deena, over and over those last years we spoke on the phone, that if anything happened to her, I wouldn't let them bury her there, in that place where she was so unhappy.

"Promise," she used to say, her voice low and fierce, "Promise you won't let them keep me there."

In the end, I didn't take all of Deena's ashes, but I took enough. Enough so that she wouldn't be stranded in that house she always hated, that past she spent her life trying to escape. After I took the ashes, I went in the bathroom, closed the door and arranged the baggies around the sink. I stared at my face in the mirror. I knew what I was going to do before I even did it. Still, I watched myself in the mirror as I unzipped one of the bags, as I held it to my nose and sniffed. It smelled chalky and dusty and before I knew what was happening, the pale flash of my palm reached down inside as I watched, fascinated and somewhat startled, as my hand made its way up to my mouth.

It was dry, pungent, with a heavy aftertaste of earth and stone and bark. My eyes watered, and I choked it down, this handful of Deena, these gritty and hard remains. I swallowed, I ate shards of my sister's bones.

***

During the long Alaska summer evenings my son and I walk the dog around the lagoon, up in the mountains, out by the inlet when the tide comes in and the setting sun turns the water silver-purple. My son runs ahead of me, legs fast, arms a blur of motion. Awkward and unselfconscious, legs so long and thin my chest flutters. He finds things: frogs, dragonflies, rocks and wood shaped by the motion of water. Shouting, stuffing his pockets, running to show me.

His face smeared with mud. Pizza crumbs in his braces. Pants ripped, socks mismatched, shoes falling off his feet.

My son, ah, my son!

***

It took me months to decide what to do with Deena's ashes once I brought them back home to Anchorage. At first it exhausted me, it was too damned much, and I left them on the dresser in the back bedroom, which had flooded from the summer rains and was waiting to be restored. For weeks, when I went in to get a fresh pair of underpants or change my shirt, I would glimpse that bag and feel a heavy weight slam my stomach.

After the room was repaired, I moved my sister's ashes to the kitchen, in the corner of the counter, next to a pile of spruce cones and the cat's ear mite medicine. I told myself I was looking for the perfect container but really, I was stalling.

It came to me one night as I was washing the dishes, the warm water soothing my hands. What I needed wasn't a vase or a fancy container or even one of those decorated urns. Deena would hate such a resting place, she would feel out of place and awkward, the way I feel when I walk into an expensive department store. No, she needed something to fill her up, nourish her. Something homey and cozy, something that would speak for all she had once wanted, and lost, and was too damned tired to fight to get back. Something that would feed her hungers.

I found it a few nights later while shopping at the Walmart with my son. "Look, Mom," he said, pointing at a row of singing cookie jars, plastic and cheap, but cute, endearing. He opened the lid of one shaped like a plastic barn, and the theme from *Green Acres* popped out. I hummed along and that's when it hit me: The farm, all those days, months, years roaming the fields and swinging across the hayloft on a rope, and that heady moment of fear before letting go, the roof boards creaking, the hay rushing toward us with an exhilaration that bordered on terror, and then scratchy hay dust in our eyes ears hair necks. Laughing. Screaming. Running back to do it again.

"I'm going to get this for my sister's ashes," I told my son, picking it up and putting it in the cart. "Think she'll like it?"

He lifted the lid and played the song.

"It's okay," he said. And then he pounced on another one, shaped like a small beach house, a high, thatched roof, a door and little window. It played the theme to *Gilligan's Island*, and I sang along, remembering how we watched that show in the evenings, our homework done, both of us sitting in the living room with our dirty feet and hay-coated hair and salty, sweaty smells.

"It's a house," my son said excitedly. "You said she never had a house, that she always wanted a home."

I brought it home, opened it up, poured in Deena's ashes, and set it on the kitchen counter between the cats' bowls and shelves of herbal remedies. In the morning, the sun slants across it, and often one of the cats curls up against it and sleeps. In the evening, when my son and I bustle around fixing dinner and chatting about our day, I sometimes open the top and we stand there, frozen for a moment as we listen to that song.

When I look at the few pictures I have of Jake, I am struck by how much he resembles Deena: the same full face, the same mouth, thin and careful, as if even when they smile, they are afraid of giving away too much. They wear a haughty expression around their eyes, that toss of a head, that turning away that comes so easily for both of them. Yet there is something so achingly vulnerable about them, something almost childlike in their innocence, in the way they hold their heads so high and allow so little in.

Did I recognize this at the time, did I seek him out because of those pieces that he kept inside of himself, untouched and guarded? Do I love him, or is it Deena that I really love, Deena that I am trying to touch and swallow all those hours and weeks and months in his bed?

He looks like her, that's all I know, around the eyes and the mouth. He looks like her.

My son stands in the kitchen cooking ramen noodles. It's late at night and he wears a pair of shorts and a tee shirt. His legs are thin and muscular, his feet flat and big. How did his feet get so big? Because it is winter, his skin is very pale. He's beautiful and almost unearthly, caught in that stage between boyhood and adulthood, standing right at the edge, ready to leap but still uncertain, still hesitating.

He doesn't know that I watch him. His face is intent as he stirs in the spice mix. He's very precise, my son, very logical and orderly. But also cheerful and playful, running around the house with the dog, hopping on his knees or pushing a ball across the living room rug with his nose. Quick to laughter, braces shining in the light. He looks a lot like his father, with traces of my own face hidden inside his. How strange to look at someone and see parts of my own self shining back.

———⁓———

My oldest sister tells me this story. We are sitting in her small, cool apartment back in northwestern Pennsylvania. Outside, the smell of the lake filters up on hot, dry winds. I sit curled on the couch while she leans on a large dog kennel she uses to take her many cats to the vet. In another room, my son plays with the kittens. My sister, her face slightly shadowed, tells me about a hiking trip in Arizona a few months back, and how she became stranded at the top of a mountain all night. She started the climb late and by the time she reached the top, it was dusk, and she knew she wouldn't have enough time to make it down. But she had her cell phone with her and she called the rangers, told them what was up, and they advised her to stay there all night, climb down early in the morning.

And so she did. My oldest sister, the most beautiful of us all, brown-gold eyes of an Italian princess, she stole the show all those years, we lived in her shadow, her round brown shadow. This sister whose beauty hasn't saved her, who is as flawed and frayed as the rest of us, though her eyes are still the same, beautiful, deep; a person could lose themselves in those eyes. This sister now hesitates in dealing with complexities and emotional changes. But she sat on that mountaintop, built a fire and huddled beside it for warmth, singing old songs to keep herself awake. She had to stay awake, she told me; she had to keep the fire going.

She was hungry, she says. And she could hear rustling behind her, animals slipping past, but this sister has never been afraid of animals, she is blessed that way. When daylight came, she called the ranger, packed up her few things in her daypack and hiked back down. It was nothing, she shrugs now, but of course it was so much more, this older sister, so much heaved upon her shoulders. She was the one, all those years, waiting up for me when I came home late from dates, sometimes slapping me across the face for being fresh. Little mother, little one, so much responsibility on her shoulders, and does it matter if she took it on willingly or had it thrust on her? It was there, it sank and shuddered and caused strange, rasping coughs in her breaths.

But she does this now, from her small apartment, her small life, we all have small lives, we are lucky that way, to have this smallness, this tiny hovel of hope and despair, and maybe she rarely writes or phones or keeps in contact with us, but she's gathering sticks and pine cones, small thin twigs for kindling. She's stoking hot ash and waiting for the flame to jump. She's keeping the fire.

⁓

I haven't mentioned much about my mother, isn't that funny? So much a part of the story, yet I have chosen to keep her hidden, surrounded by the shadows she was so comfortable hiding inside. She thought she didn't deserve much so she never tried to get away. That we suffered because of that was something she chose not to see. She told us that she married him to keep the family together. That she couldn't support four children on her own, that she was afraid we would be separated, handed out to foster families or relatives who would take us in, but grudgingly.

She taught us to do what she couldn't, she taught us we needed to get away. That was her one gift. Not how, so we did so desperately, gracelessly, but still we managed. We all left that small, sullen township. From the time I was ten, I was plotting my getaway. Always out West, in the desert or the mountains where the sky was large and blue. That I accomplished this is a small miracle. But I left, and maybe I left for the wrong reasons, but in the end that doesn't matter. I've hiked to the tops of mountains, camped beneath the wide and open sky, seen sunrises over the ocean, sunsets in valleys with no one around for miles, nothing but the wind and the beauty of my own breath.

Every moment, every hellish, god-awful moment of my past was worth the price of what I have now, the desert, the mountains, the long summer nights when the sun barely sets and I run up in the mountains, the inlet shining in the background.

I've never thanked my mother for this. It's something we can't talk about, something we both just know.

In the supermarket, my son talks about computer programs. I'm tired from a long day at work and we still have two more stores to go to. I hold a cucumber in my hand as I nod my head at him.

"Is it a template?" he asks me about one of the programs where I work. "Do they do the pages from the same template that's on your machine?"

I'm not sure what a template is but I nod, put two more cucumbers in the bag, wonder if we need more lettuce. My son is excited, his arms waving among the tomatoes.

"Then they take the pictures with a cam?" he asks, and really, I don't know what he's talking about, I'm tired, my head aches. I nod again, wheel the cart over to the corn, start tearing off the husks, remembering how we did it back home, those tall cornfields each summer, and how we picked ears for supper, kept the tassels for doll hair. The smell of corn, Deena and I pulling quickly, our feet in cheap Kmart sneakers, our legs scratched and scabbed.

"Or maybe they don't use cams?" my son asks. The corn is moldy, I can't find anything worth keeping, my head is pounding, my eyes ache, I'm ready to snap.

". . . and then format from your computer . . ." he's saying. I open my mouth, ready to ask him to please, just please be quiet. But his head is turned up toward mine, his eyes shine, he's excited, and I can't bear it, this son with his beautiful face, his thin legs peeking out beneath his shorts.

"What kind of cereal do you want?" I ask, but he ignores me and keeps talking. I wheel the cart next to him, through that supermarket with bright lights and so much food, so much to eat and buy and consume. It makes me almost giddy, the idea that I could have so much, that I've ended up with so much.

That I have all of this.

~ ❧ ~

My youngest sister is the only one I talk to on the phone regularly, the only one who flies up to Alaska to visit with my son, the one who laughs when I tell her about our life, the antics of the dog and cats. She calls my son the Young Master, and we all take vacations together, to Denali and places around Alaska, and a few years ago, Disneyland.

Ah, my youngest sister. Shorter than the rest of us, with a round face that gives her an impish look. Funny, clever, quick-witted, brilliantly smart. Growing up, we slept in the same room, for years we slept like that, in twin beds pushed against opposite walls. Falling asleep to the rhythm of her breath and sometimes now, when I visit her or she comes up to Alaska, I stand outside her room as she sleeps, close my eyes, breathe in time with her: In, out, pause. In, out, pause.

Growing up, I loved her the best. Not the most, but the best. That is why I can't write about her. Some things can't be said, some strands of love so strong and binding there are no words. When I think of this sister, my youngest sister, I imagine her standing outside in the sun, her skin soft and beautiful, the veins in her wrist purple-blue with the power of her blood.

—◦—

Jake will soon leave and move to another mountain town, thousands of miles away. I'll stay up in Alaska with my son and the long summer days, running mountains and standing in the wind with just the dog, nothing around but the trees and the sky. I'll miss Jake most at such times, in my silence, in all the things I never told him.

I fell in love with him after my sister died and rode his body in grief and anger, in betrayal and sorrow and a love so fierce I often lifted my head and howled, each spasm an anguish that pierced my veins and soul, yet somehow miraculously cleansed me. Afterward, he talked, his voice soft and deep, and I thought of clouds and the way the ground smells after it rains. Sometimes I talked too, and my voice was different then, softer yet stronger, the voice of the person I was supposed to be. He gave me so many gifts: Of sorrow and anger. Of grief and mourning and silence and hope. And the biggest one, the one I can never repay—the gift of my appetite.

What do you do, what can you possibly give back to someone such as that? You close your eyes and allow him to walk away. You don't say goodbye. Instead, you say, "Thank you." You say it softly. You say it with love and hunger and the taste of food between your teeth.

—◦—

I was a vegetarian for almost fifteen years before my sister died. But sometimes now I eat meat. Not a lot, but a little free-range chicken or salmon. I cook this up, arrange it on a plate.

I offer it to my son.

We sit in the living room and eat. The dog and cats sit beside us, waiting for their share. We are messy, eating. We don't care about manners or chewing nicely. We tear into the chicken, crunch broccoli, close our eyes to the sharp, welcoming taste of cheese. Our lips become shiny with oil, and we wipe our hands over our shirts frequently, not caring about stains.

We enjoy our food. This is what we do, then, the only thing that is left to do: We taste, we swallow. We feed.

In the dream I'm swimming with Deena. We are both still children and we wear only our underpants, our chests tanned and flat and boyish. Our hair is wet and sleek and plastered against our heads, our feet and hands wrinkled from being in the water so long. We doggy-paddle back and forth, back and forth, we are tireless, we laugh and splash and dive down deep until we reach the bottom of the pool. We play games to see who can sit on the bottom the longest. We race from side to side, and we never stop, not even when our mother tells us it's time to get out. We don't look up; we have no intention of leaving. We fill our mouths with water. We spit long and beautiful arches.

Two years after Deena dies, and it's a time of late summer rains. The windows open, rain splashing the sill. It is almost time for my son to go back to school and the air is filled with that melancholy dampness that signifies endings.

After my son goes to bed, I pace the house, ending up in the kitchen, that holy place, keeper of food and drink, smells and tastes and never as clean as it should be. I hold a razor in my hand, a pink disposable women's razor. I cut my arm, a small, dainty cut that will heal within days. I open the cookie jar that holds my sister's ashes, the faint tinkling of song filling the air. I hold my arm over that gray-shadowed place.

My blood drips slowly, slowly.

Sister, wake up.

Open your mouth.

I feed you.

This.

FILLING

Love Notes

An old Valentine from Deena's scrapbook, the paper yellowed and thin. It's a handmade Valentine, we used to get a lot of these because store-bought was more expensive. The Valentine is written in red crayon, an awkward heart drawn at the bottom, and it's from a boy in her elementary class:

I lik you Deena. I lik Laura and Beth but I lik you best.

—what I carried around in my bra for years after Deena died

Anchorage, Alaska, and Tucson, Arizona

It's been almost fifteen years since Deena died. I can barely remember her face, the sound of her voice. It's impossible to hold on to what has been lost, yet we try. It's the one thing we all do, and we do it badly and awkwardly, the way we try to keep pieces of those we once loved.

I don't know who Deena would be if she were alive, if she would have pulled herself together, started eating again, gone to therapy and taken medication for whatever type of mood disorder caused her to see things that weren't there, though maybe they were there, at least for her. Maybe it was just that no one else could see her visions, her truths.

I don't know who I would be if I had stayed with Jake. I try to imagine it, a house somewhere, small rooms filled with light, the two of us sitting at a table and behind us his music, my writing. A simple life, a quiet life.

Writing this, I imagine Deena's voice, *Cin, you can be quiet when you're dead.*

~~~

He's dead now, he died years ago. I didn't go back for his funeral. I knew my absence would be noticed and felt a momentary thrill of rebellion followed by a stab of sorrow and guilt.

Once, Deena asked me to dance on his grave, as if she knew that she'd be the first to go. Holding the phone to my ear, I imagined it all, imagined it down to the smallest detail: I'd wear a red dress and red heels, which I'd kick off as I danced barefoot over that gravestone, I'd dance recklessly, gleefully, I'd dance with everything I had, everything in me that was female—my blood, my womb, the shiny domes of my ovaries.

But that's not how it happened. After I heard of his death, I took the dog for a run along the frozen coastline, I did this in the dark, blocks of ice floating the inlet, everything white and silent. Mile after mile, the dog up ahead, the birch trees swaying like slender women. How far did I run that night, ten, twelve, fourteen miles? My mind clearing, my body taking over, my breath falling into that familiar rhythm of exertion.

When I got back home I sat in the living room with a glass of wine, even though I don't drink, I never drink. Still, I held a wine glass in my hands, that dark, rich color, those sweet and sultry smells, and then I set it on the mantel, got up, and in nothing but my underpants and sports bra, I danced around the living room, the dog jumping around before settling down and leaving me alone in my dance, alone in my tears and anger, my sorrow and grief, my guilty, god-awful triumph.

I danced for Deena and for me, for the person I was now and the girl I had been. I danced for my sisters and my mother, for my son and for the children he might someday have. I danced for all of us, and yes, goddamn it, I even danced for him.

~~∽~~

I'm married now, we've been together for years. It isn't easy. Love is difficult, and I do it badly, with little grace. Still, I try. Summer evenings, we run mountain trails around Alaska. I run in front, the sound of his footsteps behind me, the steady reminder that someone's there, someone has my back. We run for miles and miles, up in the mountains with so much wildness, so much danger, so much abundance.

Our sixth year together, we buy a townhouse in Tucson and spend winters running the river wash, sand soft beneath our feet, we run through canyons and up mountain ridges, the sun darkening our shoulders. We sit on warm rock ledges and eat gooey protein bars, we dangle our feet over the edges, we are fearless and tough, we see rattlesnakes, coyotes, bobcats, javelinas, salt sweat staining our shirts, tangling our hair.

It's disorientating at times, living in two houses, in two extremes, in two opposite parts of the country, but we embrace it all, the moody Alaska mountains, the sun-drenched Arizona desert. We are happy. We spend as much time as we can outside.

⁓ ⁓

I'll never have a normal appetite. I don't eat normally—how does a normal person eat? Food will always be my solace, my comfort, my source of love and anger, loneliness and regret, joy and sorrow. I eat because I'm hungry, because my stomach hurts, because I'm a long-distance runner and I need to nourish my body. I eat too much one day, not enough the next. I cook large meals and tuck them inside plastic containers, which I store in the refrigerator. Late at night as my husband sleeps, I open the refrigerator and stare at the containers, so much food waiting on the shelves for me, for us. Sometimes, I do this two or three times in one night. Food is my security, the thing I grasp when I'm falling, what I clutch, what I hold. It's not the way I show my love to others but the way I show my love to myself: fearfully, awkwardly, too much one moment and not enough the next.

⁓ ⁓

My mother eats with gusto now, with relish, with the enthusiasm of the lonely, the misunderstood, the hungry. I'd like to ask her why she hid her hunger for so many years, if she missed it, if it swam up late at night until all she could think of was food and flavors and the salty sting of chips against her tongue. Did it drive her mad, what she was missing, what she wouldn't allow herself to have? I'd like to ask her, but I can't. She is too old now, too frail. We don't talk that way.

Earlier this year, my mother sold the farm, which hadn't been a farm for years, and moved to Tucson to live with my oldest sister, who bought a house big enough to accommodate her. Winter months when I am in Tucson, I pick my mother up from her SilverSneakers class and take her out to lunch at Panera or the Olive Garden, her favorite restaurants, and she tells me stories about her life, stories I've never heard, stories about my father and grandmother, my aunts and step-father. About my mother's loneliness, her lost dreams, her high school days, growing up with her own grandmother, who never liked her. I listen to these stories, it's the last thing she can give me, the last thing I know to accept, not forgiveness or explanations but the broken, fragmented pieces of my mother's life.

Sometimes in the afternoons, I cook for my mother. I make the simple foods she cooked when we were growing up, chicken noodle soup or macaroni and cheese. I cut vegetables, measure spices. When it's finished, I measure it out in meal-sized containers, take it over to my sister's. I give my mother this food that I made with my own hands.

⁓

During a visit home to Alaska, my son and I hike mountains around Anchorage. It's a rainy week in July, sullen skies, trees softened with moisture, clouds so low that we're engulfed in a filmy white, it's like being in another world, as if no one exists but the two of us and the dog.

It's odd hiking with my son now that he's grown, now that he's stronger and faster. I watch as he pulls ahead, his sturdy legs, his tanned arms, his gait as familiar as my heartbeat. The last day of the trip, we hike a trail with posted warnings of an aggressive grizzly in the area. We see nothing but a few piles of scat dotted with red berry seeds. The next day I drive him to the airport, his arms strong around me in a hug, and watch his plane take off, my heart thumping, I can feel him in my muscles, hear his voice in my veins.

The following week, I see a grizzly on the same trail where we hiked. I watch it from a small ridge, watch as it runs past with wild energy, with muscular and unapologetic grace. I cry, I can't help it. It happens so suddenly, so unexpectedly. I am afraid and yet thrilled. I feel as if I am being given a gift, an undeserved and yet necessary gift. One to be both appreciated and feared.

I still think of Jake sometimes, I can't help it. I've thought of him with every man I've been with since. Maybe I chose them because they remind me of some part of him, and I chose him because he reminded me of Deena. Maybe we never get over our first loves, maybe we look for them in every other face we seek out, in every other pair of arms, in every piece of warmth and comfort.

Sometimes, when I'm tired and caught in that hazy stage before sleep, I imagine Jake and Deena and the younger version of my son and my old dog and my cats and my father and grandmother, all the people and things I've loved and lost, if not through death then through time, and they're running up a hill, a green, green hill, with the sky so big and vast in the background. A breeze blows their hair and they're running away from me, without a care.

Come back, I think, I yell, loss shuttering my throat.

But my heart pounds out another message.

It says, it sings: *Go.*

Go!

ACKNOWLEDGMENTS

It took me more than fifteen years to write *Malnourished*, and I couldn't have done it without the support and encouragement of so many people.

Thanks to the Rasmuson Foundation and the Alaska State Council on the Arts, whose financial contributions allowed me time to write; and to Hedgebrook and the Kimmel Harding Nelson Center for the Arts for fellowships and for offering quiet and safe places to work.

Malnourished originally began as my MFA thesis at the University of Alaska Anchorage. Special thanks to my graduate advisor, Sherry Simpson, who comforted and encouraged me through tough times, and to Jo-Ann Mapson and Ronald Spatz, who offered more support and encouragement than I had a right to expect.

A big thanks to Raised Voice Press editor Karen Pickell, who truly got my book, and my voice, and worked tirelessly to bring out the strongest possible version.

Thanks to Stephanie Land, for her invaluable comments at the Tucson Festival of Books Master Class; to *Anchorage Daily News* editor Kathleen McCoy, who taught me the importance of clarity and sparsity; to my former writing group: Deb Vanasse, Lucian Childs, Karen Benning, Susan Pope, Martha Amore, Don Rearden, Caroline Van Hemert, and the late T. Louise Freeman-Toole; and to my bloggy writing friends: Julie Valerie, Luanne Castle, Marie Bailey, Kevin Brennan, Mark Paxson, Carla McGill, and Carrie Rubin.

Big thanks and warm hugs to Susan Morgan, for the years of friendships and talks; Sarana Schell, for the dog walks and mountain runs; Alice Hisamoto, for the Alaska runs and races; David and Jonnie Mengel, for lifelong friendship and dog sitting; Monique Soria, for reading segments of *Malnourished* when I couldn't; John Edmonds, for teaching me to always want more; my sister Candace, who's always there for me; my son, who showed me the true meaning of love; my family, for their love and support; my husband, Mike Mitchell, who never stops believing in me; and my dog, Seriously, who loves running in the mountains almost as much as I do.

Special thanks to my late sister Cathie, for the shared love of books, the long talks, the years of friendship, and for trusting me with so many pieces of her heart.